Leadership or Servanthood?

Langham
GLOBAL LIBRARY

In recent years the world of Christian publishing has been awash with books on leadership development, many offering principles and models gleaned from the business world, often promoting charisma and celebrity status above character. This book, from a seasoned leader in the Majority World, including reflections from a lifetime of experience, cuts right across that emphasis, calling us to recognize afresh the need to follow the model of Jesus Christ – a model of servanthood, submission to his Father, with a clear sense of identity, in our case, as children of God, which is diametrically opposed to the leadership paradigm taught in many circles today. In essence, to follow Jesus means to be a servant, just like him. It is a simple but revolutionary, and even prophetic challenge which if followed, could lead to renewal of the Christian church, the reframing of our leadership development programs, and the reorientation in the thinking and leadership styles of many leaders.

Lindsay Brown
Former General Secretary, IFES,
Former International Director, Lausanne Movement

The greatest compliment I can pay this little volume is that I dearly wish I had read it and been changed by it at the beginning of my ministry rather than at the end. The fact is that this volume is a dollop of dynamite that will explode many Christian leaders out of self-importance into servanthood, thereby transforming their ministries. For Hwa Yung stands the contemporary paradigm of Christian leadership and CEO training on its head by affirming that God's way up is down. Thus ministry aspirants, even with a gift of leadership, must be trained not to lead but to submit, not to be served but to serve. The key here is character training bringing ministry aspirants into a deeply internalized spirit of servanthood, holiness of life, and dependence on the Holy Spirit. This is the great rescue operation for the modern church out of the perilous "quagmire of ambition and self-seeking." Here, dear reader, is a key also to unlock a whole new day in your own life and ministry.

Michael Cassidy
Founder of African Enterprise,
Honorary Co-Chair, Lausanne Movement

Hwa Yung has presented us with an invaluable reflection on a very relevant issue. In my years of work in mission, in Latin America, Central Asia, and other contexts, I have observed exactly what he so clearly describes in this book. The church and the Christian community in general are preoccupied with leadership abilities, positions of authority, and an ever-growing number of leadership training programs. His challenge to us to take a serious look at the biblical view of leadership, instead of the business models so widely offered, is so critical. Jesus Christ modeled servanthood for his disciples as the highest path to serving God and others. This is fundamentally important for the whole church. As the author rightly argues: leadership in the cause of Christ does not come from our striving to be leaders but is the by-product of a life of humble service to him and others . . . wherever we are and in whatever position we are called to by Christ and his body, the church. Thank you for this gift, brother and friend.

Decio de Carvalho
Executive Director, COMIBAM International,
Vice-Chair of the Executive Committee, World Evangelical
Alliance Mission Commission

My friend Hwa Yung, with whom I served for many years in the International Fellowship of Evangelical Students, has written an excellent book about what I consider some of the paradoxes of our work. In our effort to announce the gospel in universities we placed special attention in the training of leaders. The problem with this is that the aspect of servanthood among leaders was sometimes lost or misunderstood. Hwa Yung's book is an excellent reminder that the biblical concept of leadership includes an understanding of service as an important dimension of this ministry, and is a valuable resource to enrich our perception of the biblical concept of leadership and service.

J. Samuel Escobar, PhD
Latin American Missiologist,
Emeritus Professor of Missiology,
Palmer Theological Seminary, St. Davids, Pennsylvania, USA

Hwa Yung shows from Scriptures that servanthood is the genuine pathway to spiritual authority, an authority given by the transforming power of the Holy Spirit. He further argues that real servanthood is only possible when we live in obedience to Christ and are completely secure in our identity and person-hood as a child of God in the Father's love. This book is highly word-centered, supported by many wonderful contemporary stories from different cultural contexts, and filled with a compassionate spirit throughout. It has a delightful combination of serious biblical analysis, critical evaluation of current trends, and pastoral exhortation on Christian servanthood, rather than leadership. I found this book deeply moving and pray that God will use it to bless many.

Rev. Dr. Patrick Fung
General Director, OMF International,
Member of the Board of Directors, Lausanne Movement

"Oh, not another book on leadership" was the thought that came to mind when I read the manuscript title of this work. I am convinced now that we really need this book! Unfortunately, character formation has not been given its due significance and as a result Christian leadership globally has been facing one crisis after another. Hwa Yung profoundly approaches the issue of servanthood from a Trinitarian perspective. A special feature of this book is the in-depth interaction with scholarly works on theology and leadership. In doing so the author does not offer abstract theological concepts and leadership ideals but provides down to earth practical applications from his vast ministry experience. This book is not to be read but to be lived out by all who are in leadership roles.

Rev. Riad Kassis, PhD
International Director, Langham Scholars, Langham Partnership

This is one of the best books on servanthood and leadership that I have ever read! It challenges so much of conventional corporate thinking on leadership that has crept into churches, seminaries, and organizations. In an era of personality cult and the slick CEO kind of leader, this book recalls us to the teaching of Jesus and the apostles to be first and foremost disciples and servants. I loved the themes of the book, and it also challenged me to take a hard look at myself and how I lead. There is a depth about this book that is deeply rooted in Scripture and a richness that will benefit the global church. Every follower of Jesus, theological student, and Christian worker should read it!

Peter Tarantal
Associate International Director, OM International,
Senior Advisor, Movement for African National Initiatives

This significant book written by a senior Christian leader from Asia is urgently important for Christians everywhere but especially for Western Christians. So much of Western Christianity (and increasingly also elsewhere too) looks to secular models of leadership from the worlds of business and the Academy for the vision of what Christian leadership should be. The effect has been to encourage self-seeking and ambition in many Christian leaders. Hwa Yung shows convincingly that that is not what the Bible tells us to do. Servanthood, the Bible says, is both the path to genuine leadership and also the way it is exercised. Everywhere today in Christian circles there are programs on training Christians for leadership. But the New Testament never talks about how to train Christian leaders. Rather everywhere, it talks about servanthood as the fundamental characteristic of genuine Christian leadership. Hwa Yung is right that great Christian leadership is not attained by seeking it in itself. Rather it is the fruit of true servanthood modelled after Jesus Christ. The global church desperately needs to hear this message.

Ronald J. Sider, PhD
Professor Emeritus of Theology, Holistic Ministry, and Public Policy,
Palmer Seminary at Eastern University, Pennsylvania, USA,
President Emeritus, Evangelicals for Social Action

Leadership or Servanthood?

Walking in the Steps of Jesus

Hwa Yung

 **Langham**

GLOBAL LIBRARY

© 2021 Hwa Yung

Published 2021 by Langham Global Library
An imprint of Langham Publishing
www.langhampublishing.org

Langham Publishing and its imprints are a ministry of Langham Partnership

Langham Partnership
PO Box 296, Carlisle, Cumbria, CA3 9WZ, UK
www.langham.org

ISBNs:
978-1-83973-576-9 Print
978-1-83973-606-3 ePub
978-1-83973-607-0 Mobi
978-1-83973-608-7 PDF

British Library Cataloguing-in-Publication Data
A catalogue record for this book is available from the British Library

ISBN: 978-1-83973-576-9

Cover & Book Design: projectluz.com

To Bee Teik,
for the many years we have journeyed together

Contents

Preface

Everywhere we go in the church throughout the world today there is this drumbeat of emphasis on leadership and leadership training. This is true of local and national churches, colleges and seminaries, youth groups and parachurch organizations. At group discussions and seminars I have often asked the question, Where does Scripture teach or encourage leadership training in the church? Invariably the participants start scrambling all over the Bible and still end up stumped! I would like to suggest that there is not a single verse in Scripture that teaches this. The emphasis seems to have come about as a result of the church jumping on the corporate and academic bandwagons, and unthinkingly adopting it. And when we look carefully at numerous examples of church leadership throughout the world today, the negative consequences of this trend unfortunately become plain.

Despite the inclusion of the term in the title, this book is not primarily about leadership. Indeed in some ways it strongly critiques the various leadership approaches and concepts that are taught in churches and Christian organizations today. Rather the focus is on servanthood. However a clarification is in order. Many writers have in fact discussed the place of servanthood in Christian ministry. But except for the rare few, most of these writers begin with leadership and then speak of servanthood as one of its indispensable elements. The most obvious of these are the advocates of the "servant leadership" concept. However, this approach means that servanthood is invariably seen or refracted through the lens of leadership, resulting in a distortion of our understanding of the Bible's teachings on the subject. If we are to grasp clearly what biblical servanthood is about, we must look at what the Bible says about it on its own terms. Only then can we properly comprehend biblical servanthood.

The central emphasis in this book is that the call to discipleship and ministry is first and foremost a call to be a servant of Christ and the church, and not to leadership. Side by side with this emphasis is that ultimately spiritual authority for the advance of the kingdom flows out of our submission to God, just as the incarnate Jesus's authority flowed out of his total submission to his Father. This does not mean that the church does not need leaders. In fact, we are in desperate need of such today. But true spiritual leadership is exercised or results only when we have learned genuine servanthood and submission.

Chapters 1 and 2 focus on servanthood as our primary call in ministry. Chapters 3 and 4 argue that Jesus's authority is rooted in his submission to the Father and exercised in the power of the Spirit in accordance with the will of the Father. The same principle applies to us in life and ministry. But what is it that gave Jesus the strong sense of identity, security, and personhood that enabled him to persevere as a human being in obedience and faithfulness in face of intense opposition and ultimately even to the cross? It was the knowledge of and the unshakable confidence in his own identity as the "beloved Son of God" in which he was repeatedly affirmed, especially at his baptism and the transfiguration. In the same way, it is in knowing and fully grasping our identity as God's sons and daughters that will give us the security, confidence, and strength of personhood to live in submission and obedience to our Father, even in the face of pressure and opposition. These issues are addressed in chapters 5 and 6. In chapter 7 we look at the central importance of character in discipleship and leadership, and chapter 8 deals with God's work of transformation in shaping character in the lives of his servants. Chapter 9 concludes the book by pointing out that the work of the kingdom advances through those who are true servants because they carry the mantle of the Father's authority.

What I seek to demonstrate here is that the call to live out his incarnate life as the servant of God, the principle of total submission to the Father, and the clear sense of his self-identity as the "beloved Son" are three inseparable and integral aspects of Jesus's life and ministry on earth. As Christians we are called to live our lives in exactly the same way by holding together in an inseparable manner the call to servanthood, our total submission to our Father, and the knowledge – in the depth of our being – of our identity as children of God. Only by so doing can we demonstrate a way of following and serving Christ that is diametrically opposed to the obsession with the leadership paradigm currently taught and pursued by many within Christian circles, especially by those holding or aspiring to leadership positions.

I began this preface by drawing attention to the fact that the church has bought unthinkingly into a leadership paradigm that is borrowed from models in the corporate and academic world and contrary to biblical teaching. But because it appears to promise success, many serving in churches and Christian organizations, both paid professionals and volunteers, find this paradigm attractive and have often been seduced by it. This has two consequences at least. First, in many parts of the global church we see numerous examples of dysfunctional and oppressive leadership, many of which end up making headline news in the media. Second, this incorporation of secular leadership models into the church's agenda has left many, both those who are already serving in the church and those preparing to do so, with much confusion of priorities. On the one hand they know they are called to serve Christ and his church with self-giving and humility, but on the other they are encouraged, knowingly or unknowingly, to strive to be top dogs in the leadership rat race! These are incompatible priorities. Sooner or later something has got to give.

My hope and prayer in writing this is twofold. First, the apostle Paul urges Timothy, "Do your best to present yourself to God as one approved, a worker who has no need to be ashamed" (2 Tim 2:15). I trust that this volume will help the reader to strive precisely to be such a worker – the best possible for God – and yet always having the heart of a servant, not sidetracked by the pursuit of success in public eyes. Second, I pray too that the leadership in our churches and Christian organizations will be challenged to undertake a thorough rethink of their training programs and goals, so as to produce a generation of workers who will prioritize faithfulness as disciples and servanthood over ambition for leadership and positions.

This book has been many years in the making with contributions coming from various directions. Obviously there is much that I have learned from both my teachers and friends on the one hand and the "great cloud of witnesses" (Heb 12:1) that have gone before us on the other. These lessons have come through my reading as well as through personal interaction and observation. The material here also has been presented and discussed over the years both in my own country and at international gatherings. Some of the hardest lessons have flowed out of my personal pilgrimage and the failures from which I have not been spared. But the key ideas concerning the incarnate Christ and how he models servanthood for us are rooted in the careful study of and reflection on God's word. On the last point, I trust that I have been faithful to the scriptures by God's grace.

As the above indicates, many have contributed directly or indirectly to this book. You will find some of their names in the text but it would not be practical to name them all. To all of them I owe a genuine debt of gratitude. I do wish to thank especially Lindsay Brown for his friendship over many years, his encouragement along the way as I worked on this manuscript, and his determined efforts in helping me get this published. I also would like to thank all my friends who have encouraged and supported me with their pre-publication endorsements of the book. You will see their names on the front pages. The staff of Langham Publishing, who have helped me to get this book into print, have been a real delight to work with. Thank you to all of you for your servant hearts!

Hwa Yung
August 2021

A Servant's Prayer

I am no longer my own, but yours.
Put me to what you will, rank me with whom you will;
put me to doing, put me to suffering;
let me be employed for you, or laid aside for you,
exalted for you, or brought low for you;
let me be full,
let me be empty,
let me have all things,
let me have nothing:
I freely and wholeheartedly yield all things
to your pleasure and disposal.
And now, glorious and blessed God,
Father, Son and Holy Spirit,
you are mine and I am yours. So be it.
And may the covenant now made on earth, be ratified in heaven.
Amen.[1]

---

1. From "The Covenant Service," originally drawn up by John Wesley in 1755 and used by those in the Wesleyan tradition at their annual covenant renewal during the Watch Night service. This version is in modern English.

1

The Call to Servanthood

The Swiss watch industry is world renowned with names like Rolex, Omega, Longines, and others. Watchmaking began in the sixteenth century under the influence of German and French craftsmen. By the late eighteenth century, through use of mass production techniques, Swiss watchmakers were able to increase efficiency and standardization, replicating excellence along the way. Despite serious challenges from other nations, they emerged as the dominant watchmakers in the twentieth century, producing some of the finest and most sought-after luxury timepieces in the world.

In the 1950s and 1960s, both Swiss and Japanese engineers competed to produce the first quartz timepiece in the world. Seiko of Japan came out with the first quartz wristwatch, the *Astron*, in December 1969 with the Swiss version hot on its heels a few months later. The quartz watch is a much more accurate timepiece than the older mechanical watches, and much cheaper to boot. But the Swiss took great pride in the clockwork watchmaking skills that they had perfected over centuries. Consequently, they failed to recognize the threat posed by the quartz revolution. Within two decades some two-thirds of Switzerland's world-renowned watch industry was wiped out by much cheaper, but equally good, products from other countries, especially Japan.[1]

Although the Swiss watch industry has since recovered, the "quartz crisis" powerfully illustrates the danger of shortsightedness and complacency in modern industry. Other comparable examples come quickly to mind. For example, the Finnish telecommunications giant, Nokia, had close to 40 percent of the global mobile phone market in 2008. But it got caught out by its tardiness in adapting to the challenge of smart phones, which began with

---

1. See Joe Thompson, "A Concise History of the Quartz Watch Revolution," *Bloomberg*, 16 November 2017, https://www.bloomberg.com/news/articles/2017-11-16/a-concise-history-of-the-quartz-watch-revolution.

Apple's launch of the iPhone in 2007. Within a few years Nokia lost the bulk of its global market share in phones, nearly collapsed, and had to be completely restructured. Although it still sells some phones today, its primary focus is now on telecommunications network equipment.

Nokia's story is part of the much larger story of the digital revolution taking place right before our eyes that is upending the whole industrial and business world. As of 2020, of the world's ten largest corporations, seven are digital companies. The all-American big five are Alphabet, Amazon, Apple, Facebook, and Microsoft, with a combined total market value of US$5.6 trillion.[2] The Chinese upstarts Alibaba and Tencent, worth more than half a trillion dollars each, are fast catching up.[3]

The digital revolution, or the third industrial revolution, has seen these "big techs," all founded recently, demonstrating exponential growth. Meanwhile many older businesses such as high-street retail businesses and printed newspapers and magazines are collapsing. Like it or not, we are living in an "Age of Accelerations,"[4] to borrow Thomas Friedman's phrase, in which the pace of change is mind-blowing.

The same phenomenon, for good or ill, is happening in the world of nations and geopolitics. Over the past few decades we have seen many countries in the Majority World[5] imploding due to mismanagement, inefficiency, and, most of all, corruption. Yet others have grown by leaps and bounds and are now rivalling western nations in economic power and influence.

Among the latter, the best known are perhaps the Asian tigers of Singapore, South Korea, and Taiwan. Lee Kuan Yew, the first prime minister of independent Singapore titled the first volume of his autobiography *From Third World to First: The Singapore Story*.[6] Few gave Singapore, a tiny land mass in Southeast Asia without any natural resource, much of a chance when it became independent in 1965. But today it has one of the highest per capita incomes in the world. Or think of China, which was a poor struggling Third World country when

---

2. "Big Tech's $2trn Bull Run," *The Economist*, 22 February 2020, 7.

3. "Most Valuable Companies in the World – 2020," *FXSSI*, 23 May 2020, https://fxssi.com/top-10-most-valuable-companies-in-the-world (accessed 25 July 2020).

4. Thomas L. Friedman, *Thank You for Being Late: An Optimist's Guide to Thriving in the Age of Accelerations* (London: Penguin, 2017).

5. The term Majority World is used to cover Africa, Asia, and Latin America, where the majority of the world's population lives and where most of the world's developing nations are located. It is also sometimes referred to as the Global South, in contrast to the Global North that represents the richer and developed West.

6. Lee Kuan Yew, *From Third World to First: The Singapore Story* (New York: HarperCollins, 2000).

Mao Zedong died in 1976. Today it is the world's second largest economy, perceived and treated as both an economic and military threat to America's present predominance.

We could go on giving numerous other examples. Although sometimes circumstances and coincidences play a part, these do not explain everything. For example, we can attribute the amazing growth of the "big techs" only in part to the serendipitous exponential expansion of the internet because many other digital firms did not succeed. And the crises that the Swiss watch industry and Nokia went through certainly cannot be blamed on circumstances external to themselves.

Again, Singapore's growth within a generation from a poor struggling ex-colony to a world-beating economy cannot be explained without the role played by one man, Lee Kuan Yew, its first prime minister. Likewise when apartheid ended in South Africa, the whole world feared that it was heading towards a horrendous civil war in which possibly hundreds of thousands would die. Yet again, it took one man, Nelson Mandela, together with those working closely with him, to pull it back from plunging headlong into an abyss of descending spiraling violence and national disintegration by demonstrating that forgiveness offers a better way forward!

The point is that leadership does matter in whatever sphere of life we find ourselves in. And the difference between greatness and mediocrity in leadership lies in the ability to properly appraise a given situation, grasp the issues clearly, seize the opportunities before us with clarity of vision and boldness, and move our organization or movement towards higher achievements in the goals that we seek. There is always need for the very best in leadership wherever we go.

Of course this has been increasingly recognized. Just look at the proliferation of MBA and leadership studies programs in universities all over the world, as well as the number of books on the subject. But leadership studies did not just begin in the twentieth century. As it has been noted, "The study of leadership can be dated back to Plato, Sun Tzu and Machiavelli. However, leadership has only become the focus of contemporary academic studies in the last 60 years, and particularly more so in the last two decades."[7]

Given the above, many today similarly speak of the need and importance of leadership in the church. Consequently, as in the corporate and academic world, leadership courses and degree programs have been added *ad infinitum* to the curriculum of many seminaries and theological colleges. Christian book

---

7. Wikipedia, s.v. "Leadership Studies," last modified 2 June 2021, 13:32, https://en.wikipedia.org/wiki/Leadership_studies.

stores are stacked full of books on this subject. And woe betide the pastor who fails to run leadership training programs of some sort in their church.

There is of course nothing wrong with such an emphasis in itself. Leadership skills are needed at every level in the church. And the personal, ministry, and management skills taught in many of these programs are often exactly what are required of those in positions of leadership in the church, whether pastors or laity.

What is troubling, however, is the content of much of what is emphasized. The overall tendency is to speak of leadership in terms that are not very different from the way the world around us does. The language that we use, the concepts we work with, and the underlying motivations assumed in such discussions are often borrowed from secular leadership studies.

A good illustration of this is found in leadership concepts promoted in megachurch circles. Writing about Peter Drucker, probably the best-known management guru of the twentieth century, *The Economist* asserted that one result of his management theories is the megachurch.

> One perhaps unexpected example of Druckerism is the modern mega-church movement. He suggested to evangelical pastors that they create a more customer-friendly environment (hold back on overt religious symbolism and provide plenty of facilities). Bill Hybels, the pastor of the 17,000-strong Willow Creek Community Church in South Barrington, Illinois, has a quotation from Mr. Drucker hanging outside his office: "What is our business? Who is our customer? What does the customer consider value?"[8]

A month after the first article, the same magazine came out with a second, "Jesus, CEO," with the subtitle "America's Most Successful Churches Are Modelling Themselves on Businesses."[9] It goes on to state that "Willow Creek is just one of a growing number of Evangelical churches that borrow techniques from the corporate world . . . American churches have started dubbing their senior functionaries CEOs and COOs."[10]

While working in Singapore in the early 2000s, I had an interesting encounter with Druckerism in this guise. A colleague of mine was helping with an event management project for one of the megachurches there. The

8. Peter Drucker, "Trusting the Teacher in Grey Flannel Suit," *The Economist*, 19 November 2005, 68.

9. "Jesus, CEO," *The Economist*, 24 December 2005, 51–54.

10. "Jesus CEO," 51.

senior pastor's young son happened to be lazing around. Teasingly she asked him, "What does your father do?" The reply, quoting almost verbatim, was instructive: "My father is the CEO of a large corporation."

Don't get me wrong! I am not saying that we do not need good management in our churches, Christian organizations, and institutions. How often have we despaired of pastors and lay leaders who are not managing the affairs of the church properly and failing to provide the necessary spiritual and pastoral leadership to accomplish the necessary goals?

Moreover, I have already affirmed that good leadership is needed everywhere, not least in the church. Great leaders who are truly men and women of God are always at a premium. There will always be a need for biblical leaders of the caliber of Moses, Nehemiah, Daniel, Peter, Paul, and the like. And when we think of people like Martin Luther, Jonathan Edwards, John Wesley, John Sung, and Mother Teresa, all of us in our innermost being long for more of such and not less!

Called to Be Servants First and Foremost

Nevertheless, the question that must be asked is: What is the central emphasis in the Bible, and the New Testament in particular, when it comes to church leadership? What is the heart of the Bible's teaching on this matter?

It appears that the key emphasis in the Bible's teaching is that we are called first and foremost to be servants and not leaders. Until and unless that is clearly taught and internalized into Christian lives, any talk of leadership inevitably encourages self-seeking ambition. And if we are honest, all of us have seen able people who have the potential to be good and effective leaders, becoming side-tracked or eaten up by ambition and power. Consequently, they fail to achieve their full potential in ministry, becoming moderately useful at best, or hurting others and destroying their own ministries and themselves at worst.

Could this be the reason why we do not find a single verse in the Bible telling us to train leaders for God's work? That certainly is the case with the New Testament. In the Gospels, we find that Jesus's primary concern is summed up in his parting command to his followers, "Go . . . and make disciples" (Matt 28:19). The command to go and make disciples is a call to his followers to replicate in their own teaching and training ministry what Jesus had focused on doing in their lives while he was with them.

We find the same thing in the rest of the New Testament. For example, Paul's instruction to Timothy, his young understudy, to "pursue righteousness, godliness, faith, love, steadfastness, gentleness" (1 Tim 6:11) is again about discipleship and the faithful following of Christ. The book of Hebrews moves in the same realm of ideas when the author urges us to strive "for the holiness without which no one will see the Lord" (Heb 12:14). It is clear that the primary emphasis in the New Testament is on the training and development of faithful and godly disciples. Nothing is mentioned about leadership development. We will return to this in greater detail in the next chapter.

As for the Old Testament, it would be difficult for a case to be made for it to be teaching leadership training in the modern sense. Moses, for example, was referred to as "the servant of the Lord" (Deut 34:5) and in that capacity he had Joshua as his "assistant" (Num 11:28; Deut 1:38). Yet you find no mention of Moses being told to prepare Joshua as the next leader. And when the time came for Moses to exit the scene, he was simply told to hand over the leadership responsibility to Joshua who had understudied and assisted him so faithfully and ably (Num 27:18–23).

The case for servanthood and not leadership as the fundamental character for Christian life and ministry in the New Testament can easily be made. We will start with the example and teaching of our Lord, and then look at how the apostles lived that out in their lives, before finally examining how the vocabulary used for leading and serving in the church supports the argument that is being advanced here.

The Example and Teaching of Our Lord

In what scholars have called an early christological hymn quoted in Philippians 2:6–11, Paul described Christ as one "who, though he was in the form of God, did not count equality with God a thing to be grasped, but emptied himself, by *taking the form of a servant*" (vv.6–7). There is no doubt that this was the common perception of the person of Jesus in the eyes of the New Testament church. This was what he taught and how he lived.

One of the clearest examples of this is found in Mark 10:35–45 (cf. Matt 20:20–28). Jesus was on his final journey towards Jerusalem and the cross. In spite of all his efforts to help them understand the true nature of his messiahship, his disciples had either deliberately refused to accept the idea or remained pretty clueless about what would happen in Jerusalem. After all, to a man, they had all signed up as his disciples because they thought that he was the promised Messiah of Israel. They expected him to lead them in battle to drive out the hated Roman imperialists and occupiers of their homeland, and thereby establish the greater Davidic kingdom. And who else would be the members of the king's cabinet in the new political order?

It was against this background that the two brothers, James and John came to the Lord (actually they asked "Mummy" to speak for them, to be exact; Matt 20:20) with their self-serving request: "Teacher, we want you to do for us whatever we ask of you . . . Grant us to sit, one at your right hand and one at your left, in your glory" (Mark 10:35, 37). What they wanted were the plum jobs in the cabinet, to be president, or prime minister, and deputy.

Jesus's response was direct and simple: "You do not know what you are asking. Are you able to drink the cup that I drink, or to be baptized with the baptism with which I am baptized?" (Mark 10:38). Jesus was referring to the Old Testament images of the "cup" of God's wrath (Isa 51:17; Jer 25:15; Zech 12:2), which he will have to bear on the cross, and "baptism" (Isa 21:4, LXX) used in the sense of overwhelming suffering, which he would have to undergo. He was using these terms to press home the lesson on the meaning of his messiahship. But not having fully grasped what the Lord said, James and John glibly replied, "We are able" (Mark 10:39a). Or, as the hymn writer Earl Marlatt captured it so neatly, "'Yea,' the sturdy dreamers answered, 'to the death we follow thee'"![11]

Jesus's follow-up reply was not only direct but prophetic as well: "The cup that I drink you will drink, and with the baptism with which I am baptized, you will be baptized, but to sit at my right hand or at my left is not mine to grant, but it is for those for whom it has been prepared" (Mark 10:39b–41). As Jesus foretold, James would become the first martyr among the apostles (Acts 12:2) and John is almost certainly the one who was exiled to Patmos in his later life (Rev 1:9).

But the two brothers were hardly the only ones guilty of self-seeking ambition. Mark goes on to tell us that "when the ten heard it, they began to be indignant at James and John" (Mark 10:41). Why? Not because they were more virtuous and less self-seeking, but because they too were jockeying for the best jobs in the cabinet and therefore angry that the two had jumped the gun! Thus the stage is set for the climax of the Lord's teaching on the true nature of his messiahship and the gospel call to servanthood.

> And Jesus called them to him and said to them, "You know that those who are considered rulers of the Gentiles lord it over them, and their great ones exercise authority over them. But it shall not be so among you. But whoever would be great among you must be your servant, and whoever would be first among you must be

---

11. Earl Marlatt, "'Are Ye Able,' said the Master" (1926).

slave of all. For even the Son of Man came not to be served but to serve, and to give his life as a ransom for many." (Mark 10:42–45)

The above verses need no elaboration, though that would not be the last time the Lord spoke about servanthood before completing his work of redemption of the world on the cross, and thereby demonstrating in full the meaning of Mark 10:45.

John 13:1–20 tells us the story of the Last Supper. That evening they are all seated together in the upper room for supper. Everyone in the room has dirtied his feet through walking through the dusty roads. Tables used for meals in Palestine were low and seldom more than 45 cm or 18 inches high. Quite apart from personal comfort, eating with dirty feet so close to the food is just not on. A host usually provided a servant or even a slave to wash the guests' feet before a meal. But that day there is neither host nor servant. So, Jesus rises from his seat, taking on the task of a lowly servant he washes everyone's feet.

Within the strict hierarchical culture of Jesus's time, this simple act must have shocked the disciples, as indicated by Peter's initial refusal to let his feet be washed (John 13:6–8). Jesus uses the opportunity to drive home one last time what it means to follow him.

> When he had washed their feet and put on his outer garments and resumed his place, he said to them, "Do you understand what I have done to you? You call me Teacher and Lord, and you are right, for so I am. If I then, your Lord and Teacher, have washed your feet, you also ought to wash one another's feet. For I have given you an example, that you also should do just as I have done to you. Truly, truly, I say to you, a servant is not greater than his Lord, nor is a messenger greater than the one who sent him. If you know these things, blessed are you if you do them." (John 13:12–17)

Did the disciples finally get it? Yes, but only after the cross and resurrection!

How Did the Apostles See Themselves?

While Jesus was still alive, personal ambition and concerns for self-advancement had blinded the disciples from hearing and understanding what their Master was trying to tell them. But seeing him arrested, tortured, and crucified, and then finding an empty tomb and encountering the risen Lord changed everything. The New Testament records clearly indicate a radical shift in perspective.

We begin with Peter, who is always named first in the list of the twelve disciples. He took the lead naturally in the Gospels and often acted as the spokesman on behalf of the others. He was so self-confident that he vowed to Jesus on the night of his arrest, "Though they all fall away because of you, I will never fall away . . . Even if I must die with you, I will not deny you!" (Matt 26:33, 35). Brave words but – as we all know well – empty!

But that was to change in his later years. We see this in the two letters that bear his name. For example, he writes:

> So I exhort the elders among you, as a fellow elder and a witness of the sufferings of Christ . . . shepherd the flock of God that is among you, exercising oversight, not under compulsion, but willingly, as God would have you; not for shameful gain, but eagerly; not domineering over those in your charge, but being examples to the flock . . . Clothe yourselves, all of you, with humility toward one another, for "God opposes the proud but gives grace to the humble." (1 Pet 5:1–3, 5b)

Peter was still very much in leadership but the tone has changed completely. He calls on his fellow elders to exercise "oversight" without being "domineering," and not for "shameful gain." The aim is no longer to strive to be top dog but rather to "humble yourselves, therefore, under the mighty hand of God so that at the proper time he may exalt you" (1 Pet 5:6). Again, in his second letter, he introduces himself as "Simon Peter, a servant . . . of Jesus Christ" (2 Pet 1:1). It is not just the tone alone that has changed but also his very self-identity.

It is the same with the other apostles in the New Testament. John, who had earlier come to Jesus with his brother James asking for the plum jobs in the cabinet, refers to himself as "his servant" (Rev 1:1). James, the Lord's brother, though clearly recognized as the leader in Jerusalem, introduces himself as "a servant of God and of the Lord Jesus Christ" (Jas 1:1). Paul identifies himself as "a servant of Jesus Christ, called to be an apostle" (Rom 1:1).

It is instructive to note that in all the above references and others in the New Testament epistles where the apostles identify themselves as "servants" of Christ, it is the humbler word *doulos* (slave or bondservant) that is used, rather than just *diakonos* (servant). Each of them, beyond seeing himself as an apostle, came to recognize his fundamental identity in ministry as first and foremost a bondservant or slave of Christ!

New Testament Vocabulary on Leading and Ministering in Church

The case for servanthood as our fundamental identity in ministry is further substantiated by looking at the vocabulary used for leading or governing in the New Testament. Four Greek words are used a total of ten times to describe this function in church.

- *hēgeōmai*   Acts 15:22; Hebrews 13:7, 17, 24; "to be in a supervisory capacity, lead, guide."[12]
- *kubernēsis*   1 Corinthians 12:28; "administration, the plural indicates varieties of such leading positions in the ecclesial body of Christ."[13]
- *proistēmi*   Romans 12:8; 1 Thessalonians 5:12; 1 Timothy 5:17; "to exercise a position of leadership, rule, direct, be the head."[14]
- *archō*   Used negatively in Matthew 20:25; Mark 10:42; "to rule or govern, with implication of special status."[15]

The first three words are used first and foremost in a functional sense (i.e. describing the task of administrative and organizational leadership). They may be used for those who exercise spiritual authority in the church – as in Hebrews 13:7, 17, and 24, 1 Thessalonians 5:12, 1 Timothy 5:17 and, possibly, Acts 15:22. But they also may be used simply to describe the function of administrating or organizing without necessarily having overall spiritual authority in a church. This is clearly the case in Romans 12:8 and 1 Corinthians 12:28, with both words occurring in the lists of spiritual gifts.

The fourth word *archō* is used twice and in a negative sense, the context of which is the story of James and John discussed above. As Jesus describes it, "You know that those who are considered rulers of the Gentiles lord it over them, and their great ones exercise authority over them" (Mark 10:42). The reference here is to the despots and "Big Men" of this world who "lord it over" others by instilling fear, intimidating with rage, and exercising raw power to achieve their own personal agendas.

---

12. Walter Bauer, *A Greek–English Lexicon of the New Testament and Other Early Christian Literature*, 3rd ed., revised and edited by Frederick W. Danker (Chicago, IL: University of Chicago Press, 2000), 434. Hereafter referred to as BDAG.

13. BDAG, 573.

14. BDAG, 870.

15. BDAG, 140.

The fact is that the New Testament is rather sparing in its use of words for leadership that carry the ideas of having both positional status and authority over others in the church. And even here, one of the words is clearly used in a negative sense.

Instead, the two words for "servant" mentioned earlier, together with their cognate verbs, are repeatedly used to describe ministry in the church. These are:

- *diakonos* (noun)   Servant or assistant; used for deacons in New Testament (e.g. Phil 1:1; 1 Tim 3:8).
- *diakoneō* (verb)   Word used for waiting at tables and doing other common tasks (e.g. Matt 8:15; Acts 6:2).
- *doulos* (noun)   Slave or bondservant (e.g. Mark 10:44; 1 Cor 9:19).
- *douleuō* (verb)   Act as one is in total service to another (e.g. Luke 16:13; Acts 20:19).

The first term, *diakonos*, refers to carrying out the duties of a household servant and other common tasks. The second, *doulos*, is the term used for a slave or bondservant in New Testament times. Both are close to the bottom of the social ladder in the first-century world. These two words and their verbs are used about fifty times in the New Testament for service to God and the church.

The numerous times in which the words *diakonos* and *doulos* are used stand in distinct contrast to the relative scarcity of terms used for leadership and designating positional authority over others in church, even if properly exercised. Together they point us to the central focus of what ministry in the church is about. And if you find the word "servant" unappealing, you may prefer the alternative which is "slave"! The difference between what we find in the New Testament and what is often taught in our churches today cannot be sharper.

To sum up, the above examination of Jesus's personal example and teachings, the apostles' self-understanding of their calling, and the vocabulary on leading and serving demonstrates clearly that the heart of the New Testament understanding of ministry is primarily about servanthood and not leadership. Sure, the use of terms like apostles, presbyters, or elders and deacons clearly indicates that there are many who are called to leadership in the New Testament church, exercising authority over others. But what must be stressed is that the New Testament makes it abundantly clear that the fundamental nature of the ministry and leadership to which they are called is defined by servanthood, and not by position, status, and power.

All this brings us back to the Lord's words to the disciples referred to earlier – "But whoever would be great among you must be your servant, and whoever would be first among you must be slave of all. For even the Son of Man came not to be served but to serve, and to give his life as a ransom for many" (Mark 10:43–45). In the next chapter we will explore this further in the context of today's questions on leadership and leadership development in the church. But before that we need to briefly address two questions.

Two Questions

The above discussion immediately raises two questions. First, is the emphasis on servanthood the same as the idea of "servant leadership," which is now popular in leadership discussions, not least in church circles? I would like to suggest that, although there are apparent similarities, there are also fundamental differences.

Servant leadership as a concept was first introduced in 1970 by Robert K. Greenleaf in his seminal essay, "The Servant as Leader," and further developed through his widely known book *Servant Leadership: A Journey into the Nature of Legitimate Power and Greatness*.[16] The idea has been taken further and promoted by other writers, as well as by the Robert K. Greenleaf Center for Servant Leadership.

It is not my purpose to discuss Greenleaf's idea in detail here.[17] After all his proposals were originally made for leadership in the corporate world and society at large and not specifically for ministry in the church. My concern here is primarily about the latter and not the former. However, many Christians have appropriated Greenleaf's term and use it as a fundamental concept in their understanding of leadership within Christian circles. I will therefore restrict myself to some brief comments on the efforts made by some Christians to apply Greenleaf's idea to the church.

To begin with, in his explanation of the concept Greenleaf states that, "The servant-leader is servant first . . . It begins with the natural feeling that one wants to serve, to serve first. Then conscious choice brings one to aspire

---

16. Robert K. Greenleaf, *Servant Leadership: A Journey into the Nature of Legitimate Power and Greatness* (New York: Paulist Press, 1977). The original essay "The Servant as Leader" is now widely available on the internet.

17. For a useful critique from a Christian perspective, see Siang-Yang Tan, *Full Service: Moving from Self-Serve Christianity to Total Servanthood* (Grand Rapids, MI: Baker, 2006), 47–63.

to lead. That person is sharply different from one who is leader first."[18] It is important to note that Greenleaf does make it clear that "the servant-leader is servant first" and that such a person is sharply different from one who is "leader first." At the same time, he suggests that "then conscious choice brings one to aspire to lead." Stated this way, from a Christian perspective is there not an inner contradiction in his position, or at least an unresolved tension? Is it possible for sinful humans consciously to aspire to lead and still prioritize "servant first" over "leader first"? Some writers have expressed their doubts.

Duane Elmer, for example, who has done much work in cross-cultural training and consultancy, states in his book *Cross-Cultural Servanthood*:

> I don't find the servant-leader title particularly useful. The repeated use of the word *servant* apparently doesn't remind us of the type of leadership we are called to exercise. Many who think of themselves as a servant-leader aren't – which amounts to self-deception. Many are tyrants, dictators, self-aggrandizers and benevolent oppressors. What sometimes passes for Christian leadership is rather shocking.[19]

Robert Banks and Bernice Ledbetter make the same point in their book, *Reviewing Leadership*, even if it is not stated so bluntly:

> Though Greenleaf insists that a leader is a servant first and only in the wake of that service is a leader, many people in authority place the main emphasis on the second word rather than on the first . . . Ultimately they operate in ways that are not much different from those of traditional leaders. Such people co-opted the language of servant leadership for their own agendas and purposes. Sad to say, this has often been the case in the church and in many religious organizations. . . . Overall, the word servanthood is in danger of being viewed through the distorting lens of its contemporary misuse by those in authority. It is also in danger of being viewed too little in terms of its full Christian meaning.[20]

---

18. "The Servant as Leader," Center for Servant Leadership, https://www.greenleaf.org/what-is-servant-leadership/.

19. Duane Elmer, *Cross-Cultural Servanthood: Serving the World in Christlike Humility* (Downers Grove, IL: InterVarsity Press, 2006), 156.

20. Robert Banks and Bernice M. Ledbetter, *Reviewing Leadership: A Christian Evaluation of Current Approaches* (Grand Rapids, MI: Baker, 2004), 110.

Banks and Ledbetter go on to argue that though the term servant leadership moves us away from deficient models of leadership, nevertheless, "it still gets the order of the words wrong. Leadership is the key term and servant is the qualifier."[21] In contrast, they suggest that instead of servant leaders what we need are "leading servants." But surely their proposed alternative is awkward and contrived to say the least, not to mention unnecessary. Steve Hayner, a former president of InterVarsity, USA, instead goes straight to the point when he writes: "I'm not sure if I agree with leadership as the fundamental concept and servanthood as the modifier. Jesus gives an unmodified call to us to be servants – serving God and serving one another."[22]

If the earlier arguments in this chapter are correct, then surely Hayner is right. All the New Testament evidence we have before us points to servanthood as being central in the call to ministry. It is not primarily about leadership, and the term "servant leadership" merely confuses our thinking about the fundamental nature of Christian ministry. Whether it is a useful and appropriate concept to employ in circles outside the church is another matter. Within the church it only helps to muddy the waters!

The second question we need to deal with at this point is one that was put to me after I had given a presentation on the material in this chapter. If everyone in the church is a servant, where then are the leaders? This is a perfectly logical and appropriate question, and will be dealt with in detail in the final chapter of this book. For now, I will just say that great leadership in the cause of Christ is not the result of our striving to be a leader. Leadership is the result of practicing genuine servanthood wherever we are and whatever position we are called to by Christ. By living and ministering as servants, our loving and humble service will impact those around us as great leadership.

---

21. Banks and Ledbetter, *Reviewing Leadership*, 110–11.
22. Steve Hayner, "Playing to an Audience of One," *World Vision Today* (Summer 1998), 6.

2

Servanthood and the Contemporary Church

In the previous chapter I drew attention to the danger that churches are jumping on the secular, corporate, and academic bandwagons with their fixation on leadership and leadership studies worldwide. The concern here is not about whether this emphasis is appropriate for the world of business, politics, and the like. Rather the point being made is that the churches' uncritical acceptance of this tendency reveals that we have often failed to pay proper attention to biblical distinctives despite our strong avowal that the Bible is our final authority in life and belief.

Within the churches in the West we see a constant stream of books and programs on church leadership emerging. And these are often lapped up hungrily by many in Majority World churches who still look to the West for their models and agendas because of the past relationship between Western missions and their churches. Regretfully, there have been few serious voices of protest against this trend. But one scholar who has made some pertinent observations on this is Byron D. Klaus, former president of the Assemblies of God Theological Seminary in Springfield, USA.

Byron D. Klaus on the Current Flux of Leadership

Byron Klaus's address, "The Current Flux of Leadership and Emergent Church Models in the USA and Their Transmission Globally,"[1] was presented at the World Missions Briefing, Oxford Centre for Mission Studies, in 2004. He writes

---

1. Byron D. Klaus, "The Current Flux of Leadership and Emergent Church Models in the USA and Their Transmission Globally," *Encounter: Journal for Pentecostal Ministry* 1, no. 2 (Fall 2004): 25–32.

in the context of what he sees as a leadership malaise in the USA and asks what impact that may have on the churches in the Majority World.

Klaus begins by noting that studies and publications on leadership have spawned a huge industry in the USA. Much of this comes from American businesses seeking to define markets with sophistication in order to maximize sales and profit. Thus, "the massive availability of leadership/management resources testifies to a self-perpetuating attempt to respond to the cultural shifts so deeply influenced by the consumerist predisposition of American society."[2]

Klaus spoke in a context that included the fiasco of the contested American presidential election in November 2000, the corporate collapses of Enron, Arthur Anderson, and WorldCom caused by accounting irregularities, as well as the increasing revelations of scandals in megachurches and sexual abuse in the Catholic Church. Despite leadership failings at every level, in politics, business, and the church in American society, he goes on to note that, "topical fads are evident, and church leaders strain to keep up with the latest angle on leadership to make sure that they are deemed 'current' and their effectiveness in tune with the latest measurements."[3] But the reality is that American evangelicals are having problems finding leadership models that are "biblically faithful and contextually communicative."[4]

The Bible, as Klaus notes, gives many examples of God's people blindly following prevailing models in their context, resulting in leadership failures in the work of the kingdom of God. He uses the story in Mark 10:35–45 to show that, in their scramble to be top dogs in the new political order they thought Jesus was inaugurating, the disciples seem quite unable to think beyond military power and positional dominance as leadership models. As Klaus sums it up, "Jesus' simple statement, 'Not so with you' (Mark 10:43a) must have seemed as if it were from another planet."[5]

Against this backdrop Klaus urges Majority World Christians to guard against replicating models of leadership prevalent within their cultures and contexts because these are often defective, measured by kingdom standards. Adopting alternatives developed in reaction to the liabilities of these same models would not do either, as they too may be similarly compromised. In particular, he warns that this is "where an uncritical absorption of American

---

2. Klaus, "Current Flux," 25.

3. Klaus, 25.

4. Klaus, 27.

5. Klaus, 28.

church strategies and leadership priorities can be most debilitating."[6] Given that the center of gravity of the church has moved into the Majority World, he urges the emergent leaders in the global church to face this "new and exciting reality with a proactive response to its emerging Spirit-bestowed responsibility."[7]

Klaus's challenge to Majority World churches needs to be taken seriously because many in leadership positions there have traditionally looked to the West uncritically for models and answers. Many are still unaware of the grave problems and spiritual decline that churches in the West have been and are going through, and thus they continue to copy Western models unthinkingly. And our Western friends are only too happy to oblige by showcasing and exporting their latest products for Majority World consumption, for better or for worse.

As recently as the end of 2019 I was present at a dinner in Kuala Lumpur where a representative from a megachurch in the USA was introduced as having come to promote the leadership program that his church has been running globally for some years. I was rather surprised, to say the least. Did not his church make headlines in the USA and elsewhere earlier in the year because the senior pastor had to resign over sexual abuse charges? Also did not the whole eldership board resign subsequently in admission of their failure to deal adequately with the complaints that had come much earlier? And was there no recognition of the fact that there may just have been some connections between the leadership program that his church was running globally and the leadership implosion in his church? Clearly not! In any case, as they say, the show must go on!

To sum up, Klaus's address does not deal with the servanthood agenda in particular. But he is clearly drawing attention to the problem of Christians jumping onto the corporate bandwagon with its fixation on leadership and leadership studies. He also notes that many leadership models prevailing in our cultures and contexts are not consistent with the values of the kingdom. His call to Majority World Christians to do a thorough rethink on leadership models is in fact a challenge that applies equally to the church worldwide.

This brings us back to our theme of servanthood. When we think of leadership, Christians oftentimes slip into the world's way of thinking that great leaders are usually larger-than-life figures, visionaries, and commanding or even dominating personalities. Some of them may even be egocentric and self-promoting types. And often within the church, members put up with such

---

6. Klaus, 29.

7. Klaus, 29.

leaders simply because they are the boss and that is what we expect leaders to be like! But is that what truly great leaders are like? Let's turn to one careful study that challenges this line of thinking.

Jim Collins and Level 5 Leaders

One book on leadership in the corporate world that has helped my thinking on the subject is Jim Collins's *Good to Great: Why Some Companies Make the Leap . . . and Others Don't.*[8] The book is the result of a five-year study of American industry by his research team, based purely on empirical analysis, and is religion neutral. They looked for companies that had been performing at or below the general stock market for fifteen years, and then unexpectedly turned around and outperformed the market at least three times for the next fifteen years. In other words, over the same period, they had outperformed the blue-chips like 3M, Boeing, Coca-Cola, GE, Hewlett-Packard, Intel, Pepsi, Wal-Mart, Walt Disney, and the like.[9] Eleven companies made the list.

In their analysis of what made these companies great, they discovered a number of crucial factors at work in all of them.[10] It is beyond the scope of our study to enumerate them here. But significantly Collins's research team noted that all these companies had what they labelled a Level 5 leader, one who personifies the highest level of executive capabilities and "builds enduring greatness through a paradoxical blend of personal humility and professional will."[11] By contrast, "two thirds of the comparison companies had leaders with gargantuan personal egos that contributed to the demise or continued mediocrity of the company."[12] Thus Collins argues that really great industrial leaders are not the egocentric and self-promoting types who think of themselves as larger than life. Empirical findings show that corporate leaders who have really produced great results are very different people.

One example in Collins's Level 5 list is Darwin E. Smith, who in 1971 became CEO of Kimberly-Clark. He stayed at Kimberley-Clark for twenty years and turned it from a "stodgy old paper company" into the leading paper-based

---

8. Jim Collins, *Good to Great: Why Some Companies Make the Leap . . . and Others Don't* (New York: HarperBusiness, 2001).

9. Collins, *Good to Great*, 6.

10. Collins, 12–14.

11. Collins, 20. Collins's leadership taxonomy: Level 1, highly capable individual; Level 2, contributing team member; Level 3, competent manager; Level 4, effective leader; Level 5, as described.

12. Collins, 39.

consumer products company in the world, generating returns of 4.1 times the general stock market.[13] Yet, as Collins notes, few people knew about Darwin Smith and he never made the front page of the Wall Street Journal. A poor farm-town boy who worked a day job to put himself through night school at university, he went on to Harvard Law School. As Collins described it, he was a "man who carried no airs of self-importance, Smith found his favorite companionship among plumbers and electricians and spent his vacations rumbling around his Wisconsin farm in the cab of a backhoe, digging holes and moving rocks. He never cultivated hero status or executive celebrity status."[14] Reflecting on his outstanding corporate career, he simply said, "I never stopped trying to qualify for the job."[15]

It is instructive to draw up a summary list of how Collins describes Level 5 leaders in his study to help us avoid drawing wrong conclusions. Collins is not saying that Level 5 leaders had no egos or ambitions. Rather, he describes them as follows:

> Level 5 leaders channel their ego needs away from themselves and into the larger goal of building a great company. It's not that Level 5 leaders have no ego or self-interest. Indeed they are incredibly ambitious – but their ambition is first and foremost for the institution, not for themselves. (p. 21)

> Level 5 leaders are a study in duality: modest and willful, humble and fearless. (p. 22)

> Level 5 leaders want to see the company even more successful in the next generation, comfortable with the idea that most people won't even know that the roots of that success trace back to their efforts. . . . In contrast, the comparison leaders, concerned more with their own reputation for personal greatness, often failed to set the company up for success in the next generation. (p. 26)

> The good-to-great leaders never wanted to become larger-than-life heroes. They never aspired to be put on a pedestal or become unreachable icons. They were seemingly ordinary people quietly producing extraordinary results. (p. 28)

---

13. Collins, 17–18.
14. Collins, 18.
15. Collins, 20.

> It is very important to grasp that Level 5 leadership is not just about humility and modesty. It is equally about ferocious resolve, an almost stoic determination to do whatever needs to be done to make the company great. (p. 30)

> Level 5 leaders look out the window to apportion credit to factors outside themselves when things go well . . . At the same time, they look to the mirror to apportion responsibility, never blaming bad luck when things go poorly. (p. 35)[16]

When I first encountered Collins's book, what really struck me was that if we were to take the above description of a Level 5 leader and replace the words "company" and "institution" with the terms "church" and the "kingdom of God," we would have a pretty good psychological profile of what servanthood in the New Testament entails. We will return to this later.

Servanthood – Some Practical Implications

Up till this point I have argued that, for those seeking to serve Christ and his church, the primary emphasis in the New Testament is that we are called to servanthood and not to positional leadership and dominance. If this is the case, does that not also challenge us to get rid of some prevailing false ideas about Christian ministry and leadership in the church? What are some of these?

Too Much Talk About Leadership Development in Our Churches?

We noted earlier that almost everywhere in the global church there is lots of talk about training leaders for the church, especially among the youth. We find this in the local church, youth organizations, seminaries, mission agencies, and so on. If we are referring to management and leadership skills, a better knowledge of the Scriptures and understanding of the Christian faith, and the various things that youths, young adults, and seminarians should learn as part of their formation process in the church and the world, there can be no arguments about the need for such. But it appears that much of the hype about leadership development is not just about these. It goes further and emphasizes that we must train them to become eventual leaders in the church and to think of themselves in those terms. It is drummed into them that those who believe

---

16. Comparison leaders would do the exact opposite, taking credit for themselves when things go well and shifting blame to others or circumstances when things go wrong.

that they are called to be future leaders and to exercise influence must prepare themselves for that task.

As an illustration, allow me to quote from the back cover of an unnamed book on leadership, picked at random. It states:

> The person God trusts with leadership is the person He trusts to implement and fulfill *His* assignments. Christian leaders *live from* and *lead with* four common identity characteristics: brokenness, uncommon communion, servanthood, radical and immediate obedience. If you are interested in wielding a lasting influence, if you believe you are called to lead anyone anywhere, and if you believe God is calling you to something great . . . then seek these traits.

Like so many books on leadership this one has some really important and good things to say, especially on the four identity characteristics of leaders whom God uses. However the blurb goes on to urge readers to seek those traits "If you are interested in wielding a lasting influence, if you believe you are called to lead anyone anywhere, and if you believe God is calling you to something great." Stated this way, the focus has now shifted, whether intentionally or not, from seeking the four traits discussed because they are important in themselves to acquiring them so that we can exercise influence and become leaders that God will use. Thus, instead of putting the primary emphasis on spiritual and character growth, the focus has shifted to leadership development and achieving personal greatness. This is where the problem lies. How are we to respond?

I have already argued earlier that we do not find this emphasis on leadership development in the New Testament. Rather the emphasis is on discipleship and training men and women to live holy and godly lives. Jesus tells us that to be his disciple involves responding to his call (Luke 5:1–11), committing ourselves to him unconditionally even if it involves suffering and martyrdom (Mark 8:34–38), taking his word and commandments seriously (Matt 7:24–29; John 14:15), joining with him in the work of the proclamation of the kingdom of God (Luke 9:1–6; 10:1–20), and to bear witness to him (Acts 1:8). Paul makes a similar emphasis in his appeal to the Christians in Rome "to present your bodies as a living sacrifice, holy and acceptable to God, which is your spiritual worship" (Rom 12:1). Similarly he reminds Titus, another of his assistants, that Christ came for the purpose of "bringing salvation for all people, training us . . . to live self-controlled, upright, and godly lives . . . to redeem us from all lawlessness and to purify for himself a people for his own possession who are zealous for good works" (Titus 2:11–14).

Furthermore, I have argued that the focus of New Testament teachings on ministry is on servanthood and not positional status and leadership. Jesus repeatedly challenges his disciples to desist from their restless striving after leadership status and positions. We noted this in his admonition of his disciples in Mark 10:35–45 and the episode of the feet washing in John 13. Elsewhere he gently but firmly rebukes them for their constant bickering about who is the greatest by putting a child before them and telling them that "he who is least among you all is the one who is great" (Luke 9:48). And in his denunciation of the religious leaders of his day over their obsession with titles and places of honor (Matt 23:1–12), he concludes with a maxim that upends all that lies behind their obsession and striving: "Whoever exalts himself will be humbled, and whoever humbles himself will be exalted" (23:12).

Thus, the dual focus on faithful discipleship in life and servanthood in ministry represent the essential thrust of what spiritual and character formation is all about in the Christian life, and not the oft repeated emphasis on leadership development in today's church. In the whole of the New Testament there is only one verse that may possibly be read as encouraging us to seek after church leadership. In his letter to Timothy, Paul writes, "The saying is trustworthy: If anyone aspires to the office of overseer, he desires a noble task" (1 Tim 3:1). But how are we to understand this?

To begin with, although there is no strict uniformity in church leadership patterns in New Testament churches, local leadership in many churches outside Jerusalem were probably divided broadly into two categories. The overall spiritual and pastoral oversight was entrusted to elders (Greek, *presbyteros*; e.g. Acts 20:17; Titus 1:5), also designated overseer/bishop (Greek, *episkopos*; e.g. Acts 20:28; Phil 1:1; 1 Tim 3:1–2). They were assisted by a second group called deacons (Greek, *diakonos*; Phil 1:1; 1 Tim 3:8), who probably took care of the daily administrative tasks in the church.[17]

Should 1 Timothy 3:1 be read as encouraging those under Timothy to seek after church leadership and "run for office"? The New Testament scholar Gordon D. Fee, commenting on this, suggests that this is unlikely because whatever evidence we have "implies that men from among the earliest converts

---

17. See E. J. Forrester and G. W. Bromiley, "Church Government," in *International Standard Bible Encyclopedia, Volume One: A-D*, edited by Geoffrey W. Bromiley (Grand Rapids, MI: Eerdmans, 1979), 697.

were normally appointed to such position."[18] He goes on to argue that Paul's concern here is not about the person but on the position. "Thus Paul is not commending people who have great desire to become leaders; rather he is saying that the position of *church leaders* is such a significant matter, *an excellent work,* that it should indeed be the kind of task to which a person might aspire."[19]

Similarly, John Stott comments that "Paul is not condoning selfish ambition for the prestige and power which are associated with the ordained ministry. He is rather recognizing that the pastorate is a noble task, because it involves the care and nurture of the people of God, and that it is laudable to desire this privilege."[20] This verse therefore cannot be construed to mean that Paul is encouraging anyone to strive after position and status, let alone urging Timothy to get on with leadership development in the church in Ephesus.

To sum up, the New Testament nowhere encourages the restless striving after leadership so often seen today. Certainly the apostles are fully aware of the need for good leadership in the churches, but in choosing and appointing leaders spiritual and moral qualities are the fundamental requirements, as seen in 1 Timothy 3:1–13 and Titus 1:5–9. The overarching concern of New Testament disciple-making is not on leadership development but on producing faithful disciples and holy living. Those making genuine progress in this are then entrusted with leadership and oversight in the churches.[21]

The question must therefore be asked: Given the obvious needs of the church, why is the New Testament silent on the training of leaders? The reason, as already suggested, appears to be that until and unless the principle of servanthood has been internalized in our lives, any talk about leadership development invariably encourages self-seeking ambition. And there is no place for this in the kingdom of God!

---

18. Gordon D. Fee, *1 and 2 Timothy, Titus* (San Francisco: Harper & Row, 1984), 42.

19. Fee, *1 and 2 Timothy*, 42.

20. John R. W. Stott, *The Message of Timothy and Titus* (Leicester: Inter-Varsity Press, 1997), 92.

21. Gordon Fee in his commentary on 1 Timothy 3:1–7 notes that "Paul is concerned not only that the elders have Christian virtues (these are assumed) but that they reflect the highest ideals of the culture as well" (Fee, *1 and 2 Timothy*, 42). Furthermore, a good understanding of the Christian message and the ability to teach it are also clearly spelled out as prerequisites for leadership in 1 Timothy 3:2 ("able to teach") and Titus 1:9 ("He must hold firm to the trustworthy word as taught, so that he may be able to give instruction in sound doctrine and also to rebuke those who contradict it").

Ambition has been defined as a "strong desire to gain a particular objective," specifically "the drive to succeed, to gain fame, power, wealth, etc."[22] Further, the Latin root, *ambitio*, means "canvassing for office,"[23] or "campaigning for promotion."[24] It implies the desire for popularity, peer recognition, public visibility, and having authority over others. But as J. Oswald Sanders comments in his book *Spiritual Leadership*, "Ambitious people, in this sense, enjoy the power that comes with money and authority. Jesus had no time for such ego-driven ambition. The true spiritual leader will never 'campaign for promotion.'"[25]

It would be wrong, however, to suggest that there is no ambition or drive in the lives of the apostles or the great leaders of the church in the centuries that followed. But it would appear that where these people have made real Christian impact, it is because they had learned to set aside all personal ambitions for the sake of a much greater one, that of the advance of the gospel of Christ. Or to rephrase one of Jim Collins's earlier quoted statements on Level 5 leaders, "It's not that great leaders of the church have no ego or self-interest. Indeed they are incredibly ambitious – but their ambition is first and foremost for Christ and his Kingdom, not for themselves."

Too often we forget that power, popularity, and success are extremely seductive. They have the tremendous ability to inflict our egos with self-seeking grandeur and megalomaniac delusion. Both in history and in the church today, we see example after example of those who strive relentlessly for leadership, and in the process end up developing messianic-complexes for themselves and subsequently self-destructing as a result.

No wonder Thomas à Kempis, the fourteenth-century author of *The Imitation of Christ* urges upon those who seek to serve Christ the importance of solitude and silence. And his reasons?

> No man can live in the public eye without risk to his soul, unless he would prefer to remain obscure. No man can safely speak unless he who would gladly remain silent. No man can safely command, unless he who has learned to obey well. . . . Those who stand

---

22. Victoria Neufeldt and David B. Guralnik, eds., *Webster New World Dictionary*, 3rd college ed. (New York: Simon & Schuster, 1988), 43.

23. D. P. Simpson, *Cassell's Concise Latin-English English-Latin Dictionary*, 3rd ed. (New York, NY: Macmillan, 1966), 14.

24. J. Oswald Sanders, *Spiritual Leadership*, 2nd rev. ed. (Chicago, IL: Moody Press, 1994), 15.

25. Sanders, *Spiritual Leadership*, 15.

highest in the esteem of men are most exposed to grievous peril, since they often have too great a confidence in themselves.[26]

We would do well to heed such warnings because ambition and spiritual pride, which goes with it, are deadly things! That is why we need to move away from all the hype about leadership back to the call of servanthood.

CEOs for the Kingdom?

Earlier we noted, with reference to Peter Drucker, that the concept of the pastor as CEO in many American megachurches is borrowed directly from the world of corporate management. This idea has spread to other parts of the world, especially where rapid church growth has taken place in Africa, Asia, and Latin America. Because megachurches are big, impressive, and attractive to the popular Christian imagination, many, though not necessarily all, have unfortunately accepted the idea of a CEO pastor (or equivalent) uncritically. But there are at least two major problems with this.

First, the CEO concept has often led pastors to run their churches as corporate executives run their companies. Their primary concerns are defined largely in terms of control, efficiency, and productivity, the last of which includes membership numbers and offerings received. The negative consequences are serious and obvious. Often pastors end up more and more authoritarian in their leadership style. This is made worse in places where indigenous leadership patterns are strongly hierarchical. Without proper checks and balances in place, power abuses naturally abound. The resultant corruption due to this lack of accountability has sadly become a byword for megachurches everywhere, as well as for smaller churches that have adopted this practice.

Further, in some such churches there is little place for the weak and wounded because they do not contribute to efficiency and productivity. Unproductive workers are often fired unceremoniously without serious efforts to nurture them for greater usefulness. As for church members, in one case I know of, a leader simply told everyone that the church is not a hospital and that each member is expected to pull their weight. How then can those struggling in faith and emotionally broken feel welcomed and at home? And if the church is not a hospital for the poor and broken, the wounded and lame, and the suicidal and hopeless, what in the name of Christ is it? Clearly

---

26. Thomas À Kempis, *The Imitation of Christ*, trans. Leo Sherley-Price (Harmondsworth: Penguin, 1952), 50–51.

the idea of the pastor as CEO, with all its negative connotations carried over from the corporate world, runs contrary to the shepherd image of the pastor in the New Testament.

The second and bigger problem with the CEO pastor idea is that it finds no support in the New Testament. Although there was no one fixed leadership pattern for all churches in the first century, several things are beyond dispute. The closest support for the idea of a CEO pastor is found in what scholars call the monarchical bishop, where one bishop rules as head in a church or locality. But since the pioneering study of J. B. Lightfoot[27] in the nineteenth century, it is now generally agreed that the terms elder (Greek, *presbyteros*) and overseer/bishop (Greek, *episkopos*) are used synonymously in the New Testament, and that the idea of monarchical bishops was a second-century innovation not founded on apostolic teachings.

The only other examples where one person appears to have sole authority in a church are in the Pastoral Epistles (1 Tim 3:1–7; 5:17, 19; Titus 1:5–9) in which Paul gives instructions to his assistants, Timothy and Titus, on appointing elders and how to treat them. But these were unique missionary situations where Paul and his assistants had founded new churches and had to appoint leaders to provide pastoral care for the new believers.

Elsewhere in the New Testament, the terms "elder" or "overseer/bishop" when used for local church leadership are invariably plural or in a plural context (e.g. Acts 16:4; 20:17; Phil 1:1; 1 Tim 5:17; Titus 1:5; James 5:14; 1 Pet 5:1). And when it came to the biggest crisis of the apostolic church with the Jewish-Gentile issue threatening to tear the church apart, it was the "apostles and elders" who acted together in a collegial manner to resolve it, with James the brother of our Lord playing no more than the role of the Chair (Acts 15:13).

To sum up, outside of missionary situations where new churches were being founded, leadership as practiced in the New Testament was consistently team leadership in which no single person had sole, undisputed authority in the church. As Michael Green puts it,

> Leadership in New Testament days was shared. Whether you look
> at the twelve apostles of Jesus, or the "prophets and teachers" in
> the church of Antioch (Acts 13:1), or the five types of ministry

---

27. J. B. Lightfoot, *The Christian Ministry*, ed. Philip E. Hughes (Wilton, CT: Morehouse-Barlow, 1983). Lightfoot's essay was first published in 1868 as an excursus to his commentary on the Epistle to the Philippians and has been reprinted since in various editions.

characterized as Christ's gifts to the church (Eph 4:11), the message is the same: Christian leadership is . . . shared leadership.[28]

The rationale for this appears to be quite plain. As the famous saying of Lord Acton goes, "Power tends to corrupts, and absolute power corrupts absolutely."[29] Given the reality of our sinful human condition, none can hold power without being corrupted by it in some manner. The only way to safeguard ourselves and the church is to put in place adequate checks and balances, whereby leaders hold each other accountable in a collegial manner. Thus the pastor as the CEO concept is completely foreign to the New Testament.

What Goal Should We Set for Ourselves in Our Ministry?

Whether we are in full-time ministry working in the church or a Christian organization, or whether we are serving in a voluntary capacity, there is the natural desire as we grow to move on in the direction of greater usefulness. In itself, there is nothing wrong with this. After all, Paul was urging Timothy to do the same when he wrote, "Do your best to present yourself to God as one approved, a worker who has no need to be ashamed rightly handling the word of truth" (2 Tim 2:15). But this desire to be more useful, unless sanctified by the Holy Spirit, can be easily overtaken by personal ambition.

Given the danger that this poses for sinful humanity, what goal should we then set for ourselves in ministry? How do we strive for increasing usefulness in a manner that is right and proper without at the same time falling to the temptation of ambition and power? Two things are needful. First, whatever our position or office may be, our primary concern should always be to serve Christ and others by discharging humbly and faithfully the responsibilities inherent therein. Our primary focus should always be the job at hand and never be about seeking promotion to higher office. That is what servanthood entails.

Second, in our aspiration to be of increasing usefulness in the cause of Christ we must always fight against all conscious or subconscious attempts at self-promotion, never forgetting that this is a lifelong battle. Whereas in many traditional cultures and Christian teaching modesty is encouraged, regretfully much of the world today thrives on ambition and celebrity status. But if Jim Collins's description of Level 5 leadership is right, then we have to say that even in the corporate world the best leaders are not the self-promoting types.

---

28. Michael Green, *Freed to Serve* (London: Hodder & Stoughton, 1983), 126.

29. "Lord Acton writes to Bishop Creighton (1887)," Online Library of Liberty, https://oll. libertyfund.org/quotes/214.

Taking such an approach will probably mean that, humanly speaking, we will lose out at times to those who are wiser in the ways of the world and know how to campaign for their own advancement. Yet sooner or later, those around us and over us will inevitably recognize the spiritual quality and depth of character for what they are and seek us out for leadership and greater responsibility in the work of the kingdom. As Paul tells young Timothy, "So also good works are conspicuous, and even those that are not cannot remain hidden" (1 Tim 5:25). We should therefore simply do as Paul admonishes Timothy, which is to "do our best to present ourselves to God as one approved," and to leave the question of whether or not we move up the ladder in our church or organization entirely in God's hands.

In connection with this, we need to examine an idea advanced by the leadership studies guru, John Maxwell. In an earlier book, *The 21 Indispensable Qualities of a Leader*, Maxwell includes servanthood as one of them, and he subtitles this quality as "to get ahead, put others first."[30] It is difficult to avoid the conclusion that something here is out of sync with biblical thinking because the reason given for why we "put others first" is "to get ahead." But as a corrective, Siang-Yang Tan in his book *Full Service* asserts that "We should put others first period!"[31]

Regretfully, in a later piece in *Christianity Today* Maxwell continues to argue along a similar line: "You don't strive to be a leader, you strive to add value to people, and they'll let you be the leader."[32] Here again it is difficult to avoid the conclusion that there is a strong element of self-interest in what he advocates. So why do you strive to add value to others? In order that they will let you be the leader! If Maxwell is serious about genuine servanthood, he needs to rephrase drastically what he says: You don't strive to be a leader, you strive to add value to people, *irrespective of whether or not they want you to be the leader*. That is true servanthood.

What Goal Should We Seek in the Training of Those under Us?

This brings us to the final question. What goal do we seek in our training and discipling processes for those under us? The church needs good leaders,

---

30. John Maxwell, *The 21 Indispensable Qualities of a Leader* (Nashville, TN: Thomas Nelson, 1999), v–vi; cited by Siang-Yang Tan, *Full Service: Moving from Self-Serve Christianity to Total Servanthood* (Grand Rapids, MI: Baker, 2006), 58.

31. Tan, *Full Service*, 58.

32. John Maxwell, "Add Value," *Christianity Today Leadership Weekly*, 7 July 2002, https://www.christianitytoday.com/pastors/2007/july-online-only/le-2002-cln20725.html.

no doubts about that. Yet it is often cluttered with the wrong kind of leaders and we see failings all around. For example, we sometimes find that those who have taken on senior leadership of large mission organizations or whole denominations lack the spiritual depth and the necessary skills for effective delivery. Others may be pastors of medium size churches or ministries and are failing because they simply lack sufficient administrative and ministry skills, even if they have the aptitude and commitment. Or again, I am working right now with an indigenous rural church where all the pastors have completed only primary school education before being given some basic theological training, but among their congregations many have already graduated from high school and a few have tertiary education. So these pastors are actually finding themselves quite out of their depth.

There is clearly a need for us to do our best to help those at various levels of ministry, whether full-time or part-time, in spiritual formation and in skill acquisition. However, given the human propensity for sin and self-seeking, throughout this process we must always be on our guard against the temptations of ambition and personal advancement. This is especially so when the training also comes with academic qualifications. Difficult as it appears, we must find means to carry out this task in such a manner that we do not help fuel self-seeking ambition at the same time. It appears that the only way forward is always to put spiritual growth and servanthood at the heart of all our discipling and training processes.

Here a word of wisdom from the late Bishop Stephen Neill, missionary statesman and scholar, seems appropriate. With the colonial era fast coming to an end in the post-World War II period, there was an urgent need to hand over leadership to nationals in the emerging churches in Africa and Asia. Many mission agencies and churches were scrambling to produce indigenous leaders for this role. Against this background, Neill issued a corrective and warning. He wrote,

> If we set out to produce a race of leaders, what we shall succeed in doing is probably to produce a race of restless, ambitious and discontented intellectuals. To tell a man he is called to be a leader is the best way of ensuring his spiritual ruin, since in the Christian world ambition is more deadly than any other sin, and, if yielded to, makes a man unprofitable in the ministry. The most important thing today is the spiritual, rather than the intellectual, quality of

those indigenous Christians who are called to bear responsibility
in the younger churches.[33]

Many in the Majority World who have lived through that era, or under the
leadership of some church leaders who emerged at that time, will bear witness
to the wisdom of Neill's words.

I still remember vividly when Neill, then in his late seventies, spoke at
the college chapel when I was studying theology. His theme was what is the
goal of a theological college? His unequivocal answer was that the goal of
theological training is not to develop leaders but to produce godly men and
women. He went on to add that if God then gives the gift of leadership to such
godly individuals we can all rejoice together in it. And being the typical polite
British gentleman that he was, he held back from stating the obverse, which
is that if the ungodly takes leadership, both the church and her members will
suffer for it. He ruffled some feathers that day, especially among the faculty.
But he is right.

---

33. Cited in Sanders, *Spiritual Leadership*, 148.

3

Whence Spiritual Authority?

How can a person whose fundamental disposition in life is that of a servant still have the authority needed for effective ministry and power to change lives and the world? Surely that is a non-starter! Common wisdom tells us that change and transformation come through leaders with the power and authority to make a difference. That is what leaders do and that is why they are needed.

I must admit that was where my own thinking began in earlier days. And this is of course how the world and, unfortunately, much of the church think. My change in understanding began many years ago when I first heard a sermon on the subject by the late Douglas McBain, then a senior Baptist minister in Britain and one-time president of the Baptist Union. He was also a founding member of Fountain Trust, the inter-denominational group that led the charismatic renewal in Britain in the 1960s and 70s.

What McBain asserted in his sermon was very simple. Based on what the New Testament teaches, he simply argued that the secret of Jesus's authority lies in his total submission to his Father. Nothing more, nothing less. Over the years I have studied the Bible much more closely and am convinced that he is absolutely right. In this chapter we will examine what he said in greater detail.

Authority and Power

Authority carries with it the power to change lives, organizations, and situations. This is what we usually mean when we think of leadership. Authority and power come in various forms.

Hard Power Versus Soft Power in Realpolitik

Joseph S. Nye Jr., former dean of Harvard's Kennedy School of Government, in an address at the Center for Public Leadership's conference on Misuses of Power: Causes and Corrections in 2004, drew attention to the difference between hard and soft power in international politics.[1] Hard power is usually defined as having the capabilities or resources to shape desired outcomes. In international relationships this is linked with abundance of resources, economic strength, size of population, military force, and the like. Power in this sense is more concrete, quantifiable, and predictable. Hard power is thus clearly coercive.

Soft power is the ability of one nation to get its desired outcomes using less tangible means like attracting others to admire its values and successes, and to aspire towards its strengths and level of prosperity. Soft power is also regularly practiced in democracies with political leaders canvassing support through presenting themselves as attractive personalities, promoting desirable values, causes and institutions, and appeal based on credibility and legitimacy. Thus, soft power co-opts rather than coerces people.

In international relationships, hard power is used to command or coerce behavior in others whereas soft power co-opts or attracts them to do what we want. The types of behavior between command and co-option range along a spectrum from coercion at one end to pure attraction at the other. Along this spectrum, there is a constant interplay between hard and soft powers, sometimes reinforcing and sometimes obstructing each another. Nye further comments

> In the business world, smart executives know that leadership is not just a matter of issuing commands, but also involves leading by example and attracting others to do what you want . . . Soft power has always been a key element of leadership . . . Skillful leaders have always understood that attractiveness stems from credibility and legitimacy. Power has never flowed solely from the barrel of a gun; even the most brutal dictators have relied on attraction as well as fear.[2]

---

1. Joseph S. Nye Jr., "The Benefits of Soft Power," Harvard Business School, Working Knowledge, 2 August 2004, https://hbswk.hbs.edu/archive/the-benefits-of-soft-power.
2. Nye Jr., "Benefits of Soft Power."

Nye's address was directed primarily at international politics. But as the above quotation shows, they also have a direct relevance to our discussion on ministry and leadership in churches and Christian organizations.

Institutional Authority Versus Personal Moral Authority in Leadership

Within the church at least two kinds of authority can be distinguished. The first is institutional authority, which is the exercise of the executive powers of one's office and position within an organization. Depending on how a church is structured executive power rests with different offices. It may be the board of elders, the pastor in charge, or the bishop, and so forth. The persons with the power of the office can command obedience, although they may choose not to. This type of authority is similar or equivalent to the "hard power" that Nye speaks of and, if improperly exercised, is not only coercive but also becomes abusive.

The second type of authority is primarily personal and moral, more like the soft power that Nye speaks about in politics. It is partly based on one's personality and ability to attract others to your cause, and consequently the power to inspire commitment or a following. Ultimately it goes back to the quality of one's spirituality and life, to a person's character, personal integrity, and moral standing in the community. In Nye's terms, personal moral authority does not operate by command and coercion but by attraction and co-option.

These two kinds of authority and power are not exercised in isolation from one another. Usually they overlap and work in combination, and the respective emphases given to each vary with the person concerned. There are two things we need to note.

First, there is a natural tendency among many in leadership to prioritize institutional authority over personal moral authority, leading them to strive for the former more than the latter. We see this all too often in the behind the scenes politicking and maneuvering, especially come election times in church and elsewhere. The reason is that institutional authority is much more concrete and clearly defined. In the eyes of the world, it is linked with position, power, and status, and thus more desirable. Personal moral authority is far less tangible, being closely linked with virtue, character, and personal maturity. It is attained only through earnest self-cultivation and serious moral effort on the one hand and the work of the Holy Spirit in our inner being on the other. The worldly-wise would therefore naturally gravitate towards institutional authority rather than personal moral authority because it appears much more easily attainable and desirable. After all, you do not get a pay rise by becoming more virtuous and holy – you get one by moving up the hierarchical ladder.

The above leads to the second thing that needs noting. Nye's address referred to earlier is titled "The Benefits of Soft Power." He points out that a nation that prioritizes the employment of hard power at the expense of soft power often fails to demonstrate credibility and legitimacy in the pursuit of its goals. In doing so, it ends up paying a much higher price in terms of blood and money to achieve its desired goals, if it succeeds at all. In like manner, when a church or organizational leader fails to demonstrate character, integrity, and compassion in leadership, and merely resorts to the use of raw executive power to get things done, they often do not get what they want. Even if they do get what they want, the way they go about achieving it may actually further undermine their credibility and legitimacy. It is an extremely sad sight to behold when church leaders operate primarily on the basis of command and coercion. Everyone else can see the hollowing out of integrity and credibility in their lives.

To sum up, those called to organizational and church leadership have been entrusted with certain institutional authority, which they must exercise responsibly and with accountability. At the same time, this exercise of institutional and executive authority must be undergirded by a personal and moral authority, which is inseparably linked to character, integrity, and spiritual maturity. It would therefore be foolhardy to seek after position and institutional authority when one is not ready for it because it would only undermine one's own credibility and integrity as a person and a servant of Christ.

The Abuse of Power

While exercising institutional authority without a sufficient undergirding of personal and moral authority in oneself is a major problem, there is the related issue of power abuse in the church. This relates to the use of both institutional authority and personal authority, or to some combination of the two.

Power abuse is found in all churches of whatever denominations, theology, and polity all over the world. For example, it often happens when a church gives CEO powers to the pastor without proper checks and balances to their authority. On the other hand, even when the checks and balances are there, many a manipulative leader has learned the fine art of side-stepping them. Furthermore, in cultures where age, social status, and hierarchy take priority over the checks and balances that are in place, some churches end up with very controlling pastoral leaders. We find these, for example, in parts of the Majority

World where "Big Man" ideas prevail, or in various societies in East Asia where Confucian traditions are strong and hierarchical patents are the norm.

Power abuse does not merely result from personal failings of leaders and alien cultural patterns brought into the church. Another major source is false teachings. For example, in modern Chinese church history one well-known leader taught that, because Christians should not idolize money, all Christians must "hand over" what they have to the church for the gospel's advance. You can imagine who takes control of everything! A similar example is the now-discredited "Shepherding movement" in the US in the 1970s and 1980s, which required strict submission by everyone to someone above them within a pyramidal leadership structure going all the way to the top. This led to many members losing their self-confidence to make even simple life decisions for themselves. A third example is found in some Pentecostal-charismatic circles, wherein leaders when called to accountability over power and financial abuses, reply with the oft misquoted, "Touch not [the Lord's] anointed" (Ps 105:15)!

The above cases are examples of what happens when self-interest and false teachings take over, resulting in much of the leadership failure in the church both in history and today. Needless to say, we will be familiar with other examples of such abuses as well. On the other hand, we are also aware of many wonderful examples of God's servants ministering with tremendous spiritual authority and power. We will now explore this in greater detail.

Spiritual Authority

Though many have failed in leadership or are unable to demonstrate genuine authority in life and ministry, there have been others both in history and the present who have exercised spiritual authority of a different order. We see this first in the apostles like Peter whose one sermon at Pentecost brought 3000 to faith in Christ (Acts 2:41). We see the same in Paul's ministry when he describes Christ working through him "to bring the Gentiles to obedience – by word and deed, by the power of signs and wonders, by the power of the Spirit of God – so that from Jerusalem and all the way around to Illyricum I have fulfilled the ministry of the gospel of Christ" (Rom 15:18–19).

Fast forward to more recent times and think about some modern apostolic figures. Consider the ministry of William Wadé Harris (1860–1929), better known as Prophet Harris, who in eighteen months of ministry, from July 1913 to January 1915, in Liberia, Cote d'Ivoire and Ghana, brought some 200,000 to faith and baptized more than 100,000.[3] A comparable figure in Asia would be John Sung (1901–1944), considered by many to be the greatest evangelist and revivalist of China in the first half of the twentieth century. From 1927 to 1940, his ministry sparked revival in hundreds of Chinese churches in China and Southeast Asia, brought healing to thousands of sick people, and led some 100,000 people to faith in Christ.[4]

Nor is this spiritual authority restricted to evangelism, revivals, and the miraculous. Within global evangelicalism, many would agree that the late John Stott (1921–2011) ranks as one of the greatest teachers of the global church in the latter half of the twentieth century and the beginning of the twenty-first. His teaching authority and prophetic insights on the global church continue to impact countless lives today. Or consider the impact of Pope John Paul II (1920–2005), the first non-Italian pope in five centuries. While still Archbishop of Krakow, amongst other things, he so strengthened the Polish church that it was a bulwark against Communist totalitarianism under which it existed. And after becoming Pope in 1978, he took the same stand against Soviet hegemony until the Iron Curtain finally fell with the collapse of the Berlin Wall in November 1989. It was Mikhail Gorbachev, the Soviet leader who oversaw the peaceful transition of Eastern Europe and the Soviet Union into democratic states, who said in 1992: "Everything that happened in Eastern Europe in these few years would have been impossible without the presence of this pope and the important role – including the political role – that he played on the world stage."[5]

Earlier we had looked at the two different types of authority at work in leadership, distinguishing between institutional authority and personal moral authority. Both are important. Nevertheless, it should be noted that of the figures just described, most of them had little or no institutional authority, with the exception of Pope John Paul II. Yet there can be no doubting that

---

3. Gordon MacKay Haliburton, *The Prophet Harris* (New York: Oxford University Press, 1973); David A. Shank, *Prophet Harris, The "Black Elijah" of West Africa* (Leiden: Brill, 1994), and "The Legacy of William Wadé Harris," *International Bulletin of Missionary Research* 10, no. 4 (1986): 170–76, reproduced in https://dacb.org/stories/liberia/legacy-harris/.

4. Leslie T. Lyall, *John Sung: Flame for God in the Far East* (London: OMF, 1956), reissued as *A Biography of John Sung* (Singapore: Armour, 2004); Levi Sung, ed., *The Diary of John Sung: Extracts from His Journals and Notes* (Singapore: Genesis Books, 2012); and Lim Ka-Tong, *The Life and Ministry of John Sung* (Singapore: Genesis Books, 2012); Song Shangjie, "John Sung," in *Biographical Dictionary of Chinese Christianity* (Global China Center, 2005–2020), http://bdcconline.net/en/stories/sung-john.

5. Cited in David Aikman, *Great Souls: Six Who Changed the Century* (Nashville: Word, 1998), 258, and for details see 255–59. See also George Weigel, *Witness to Hope: The Biography of Pope John Paul II* (New York, NY: HarperCollins, 2001), 605–12.

they exercised great authority. It is not just their own personal moral authority that we see but something much more. Personal moral authority, for example, cannot empower us to do signs and wonders or bring tens and hundreds of thousands to faith in Christ. We are speaking here of spiritual authority, a unique kind of authority given in Christ, that goes beyond both institutional and personal moral authority.

We may no doubt immediately conclude that this is the power of the Holy Spirit that was promised by our Lord Jesus. After all, did not Jesus say to the disciples before his ascension, "All authority in heaven and on earth has been given to me" (Matt 28:18)? The clear implication of these words is that the disciples are called to take Christ's authority and "Go therefore and make disciples of all nations" (28:19). The same point is made in Jesus's words in Acts 1:8: "But you will receive power when the Holy Spirit has come upon you, and you will be my witnesses in Jerusalem and in all Judea and Samaria, and to the end of the earth." To link spiritual authority with the empowering of the Holy Spirit as promised by our Lord is certainly correct. But I would like to suggest that this is only part of the answer to the question where does spiritual authority come from. I believe that the complete answer is found in a proper understanding of Jesus's exercise of authority in his incarnate state. It is to this that we will now turn.

The Authority of Jesus

The four Gospels make quite clear that Jesus in his earthly ministry exercised spiritual authority of the highest order. Just a quick reading of the first few chapters of Mark, probably the first Gospel to be written down, makes this clear.

Jesus's Authority as Seen in the Gospels

Shortly after his ministry began Mark tells us that Jesus goes to the synagogue in Capernaum and starts teaching. The congregation is electrified, "for he taught them as one who had authority, and not as the scribes" (Mark 1:22). Immediately there and then he carries out an exorcism on a demonized man. The reaction is even stronger, "And they were all amazed, so that they questioned among themselves, saying, 'What is this? A new teaching with authority! He commands even the unclean spirits, and they obey him'" (1:27). By evening, the whole town gathers for his ministry: "And he healed many who were sick with various diseases, and cast out many demons. And he would not permit the demons to speak, because they knew him" (1:34).

In the next few chapters of Mark's Gospel, the account of Jesus's impact is further amplified. He heals the paralytic who is let down through the roof. He begins with the words, "Son, your sins are forgiven" (2:5), and then follows up with, "I say to you, rise, pick up your bed, and go home" (2:11). Next he heals a man with a withered hand on the Sabbath. In so doing, he upsets the religious authorities enough to want to get rid of him because he had challenged their legitimacy (3:1–6). In the next chapter, he stills a storm and provokes the disciples to ask, "Who then is this, that even the wind and the sea obey him" (4:41)? Mark goes on to recount the raising of Jairus's daughter from the dead (5:21–43). And along the way a woman suffering from unstoppable menstrual bleeding is healed just by touching him.

We find similar accounts in the rest of Mark and the other three Gospels. He demonstrates his authority in evangelism, teaching, prophetic utterances, healing and deliverance, and various signs and wonders. He further manifests his authority through his repeated confrontations with the religious authorities over their wrong understanding and application of God's law, which was leading the Jews into spiritual bondage instead of freedom. It is also seen in his socio-political critiques exemplified by his calling Herod "that fox" (Luke 13:32) and the cleansing of the temple (Matt 21:12–17; John 2:13–17). All this leads E. V. Rieu, a classicist, to sum up his personal feelings upon completion of his translation of the four Gospels with the comment, "Superimposed on all my previous impressions is one of power, tremendous power, utterly controlled."[6]

What Is the Source of Jesus's Authority?

Where did this authority and power come from? Simplistic answers will not do. The nineteenth-century German liberal theologians would like to think of Jesus as a religious genius, perhaps even the greatest religious teacher of all time. But if the above summary of Jesus's authority is correct that will not do. Even geniuses cannot raise the dead or be described as having "power, tremendous power, utterly controlled."

Another answer that is often given by the enfeebled type of Christianity I grew up with is that Jesus is God and therefore able to exercise divine powers, unlike us who are human and weak. This type of answer is still prevalent in many segments of the church wherein the power of the Holy Spirit is not properly understood and taught. In contrast to this, in many Pentecostal-

---

6. E. V. Rieu, *The Four Gospels: A New Translation from the Greek* (Baltimore, MD: Penguin: 1953), xxxi.

charismatic sections of the global church and among many indigenous churches in the Majority World, this answer will simply be laughed out of court. Indeed, the tremendous growth of the church in the Majority World in the last hundred plus years have been and still is being often driven by the manifestation of the Holy Spirit's power in healing and deliverance ministries, and in signs and wonders.[7]

Moreover, the answer that only Jesus can exercise such powers because he is divine runs contrary to his clear assertion otherwise: "Truly, truly, I say to you, whoever believes in me will also do the works that I do; and greater works than these will he do, because I am going to the Father" (John 14:12). Many Christians, including evangelicals who claim to take the Bible seriously, have simply side-stepped this verse when they suggest that we should not be expecting God to do miracles today. But the notable New Testament scholar D. A. Carson would have none of that. Instead he rightly comments, "The promise is staggering: the person with such faith, Jesus says, *will do what I have been doing*. Indeed, *he will do even greater things than these* – not because he is greater, but *because I am going to the Father*."[8] Whatever else this verse points to, Carson further adds, "Jesus' 'works' may include more than his miracles; they never exclude them."[9]

This brings us back once more to the question, where did Jesus's authority and power come from? The Bible gives a two-part answer. The first is that the authority seen in his ministry comes from the power of the Holy Spirit working through him; the second is that he did all that he did on his Father's authority. Both of these need unpacking.

Jesus the Spirit-filled man

On the first answer from the Bible, all four of the Gospels are unanimously and absolutely clear that Jesus's ministry only began after his baptism at Jordan and the descent of the Spirit upon him. Luke provides the most details. Against the backdrop of John the Baptist's public ministry at the Jordan, awaiting the

---

7. For readers who would like to know more about the modern growth and shape of Christianity in the Majority World, see for example Philip Jenkins, *The Next Christendom: The Coming of Global Christianity*, 3rd ed. (Oxford: Oxford University Press, 2011), and *The New Faces of Christianity: Believing the Bible in the Global South* (Oxford: Oxford University Press, 2006); and Lamin Sanneh, *Whose Religion is Christianity: The Gospel Beyond the West* (Grand Rapids, MI: Eerdmans, 2003), and *Disciples of All Nations: Pillars of World Christianity* (Oxford: Oxford University Press, 2008).

8. D. A. Carson, *The Gospel According to John* (Leicester: Inter-Varsity Press, 1991), 495.

9. Carson, *Gospel According to John*, 495.

manifestation of the coming Messiah, Jesus comes forward to be baptized. As Jesus prays, "the heavens opened, and the Holy Spirit descended on him in bodily form, like a dove; and a voice came from heaven, 'You are my beloved Son; with you I am well pleased'" (Luke 3:21–22). This is followed by the temptation narrative, but the way that Luke describes it is important: "And Jesus, full of the Holy Spirit . . . was led by the Spirit in the wilderness for forty days, being tempted by the devil" (4:1–2). Only after being empowered by the Spirit does Jesus go forth to do battle with Satan. Following his victory against satanic temptation, "Jesus returned in the power of the Spirit to Galilee, and a report about him went through all the surrounding country" (4:14).

Let me recapitulate. John is preaching and baptizing at the Jordan. Jesus appears on the scene and is baptized, and the Spirit comes upon him in an unmistakable manner. Then and only then could Jesus, filled with the Spirit, go forth to defeat Satan. Thus empowered by the same Spirit he returns to begin his public ministry with immediate impact, as the above discussion on Mark's account shows. No wonder Luke goes on to state in his account that the whole of Galilee was abuzz with excitement about him! To sum up, there can be no doubt from the Gospel accounts that his authority was exercised through the power of the Spirit who had descended on him at his baptism.

Jesus the Son fully submitted to the Father

We come now to the second of the Bible's answer on the source of Jesus's authority. For this we have to turn to the Gospel of John. Here we find something that may appear utterly perplexing and incredible to the world. In this Gospel, we find Jesus making a series of statements that simply says that he, as the Second Person of the Trinity, had no authority of his own but that in his incarnate state he was totally dependent on the Father. Allow me to list the most explicit.

> So Jesus said to them, "Truly, truly, I say to you, *the Son can do nothing of his own accord, but only what he sees the Father doing. For whatever the Father does, that the Son does likewise.* For the Father loves the Son and shows him all that he himself is doing." (John 5:19–20a)

> "*I can do nothing on my own.* As I hear, I judge, and my judgment is just, because I seek not my own will but the will of him who sent me." (5:30)

> "For I have come down from heaven, not to do my own will but the will of him who sent me." (6:38)

So Jesus said to them, "When you have lifted up the Son of Man, then you will know that I am he, and *that I do nothing on my own authority, but speak just as the Father taught me.* And he who sent me is with me. He has not left me alone, *for I always do the things that are pleasing to him.*" (8:28–29)

"*For I have not spoken on my own authority, but the Father who sent me has himself given me a commandment – what to say and what to speak.* And I know that his commandment is eternal life. *What I say, therefore, I say as the Father has told me.*" (12:49–50)

"He has no claim on me, but *I do as the Father has commanded me, so that the world may know that I love the Father.*" (14:30c–31)[10]

Apart from these, there are other verses that move in the same realm of ideas, even if sometimes they do so less explicitly. These include John 4:34; 10:37–38; 15:10; and 17:4. The thrust of these verses can be summed up as follows: Jesus says that as the Son he could do or say nothing on his own authority, but only what the Father commands; that he had come to earth to do not his own will but what the Father wills; and that the Son seeks to do only that which pleases the Father so that the world will know that he loves the Father.

In other words, what Jesus is asserting is that in his incarnate state while on earth he lives in total obedience to the Father, as the perfect Son. Because he lives in total submission, he cannot exercise his will independently of the Father's will. His will is at one with the Father's and he does only what his Father commands.[11] And all that he does is carried out with the Father's divine

---

10. Emphasis added in all the above quotations.

11. Readers who are not familiar with the theological intricacies of the doctrine of the Trinity and functional subordination (as opposed to ontological subordination) among the three persons of the Godhead may be perplexed by the apparent paradox so clearly stated in John's Gospel. How can Jesus be co-equal with the Father and yet totally subordinate to him at the same time? Probably the best statement on how this paradox is resolved is that by C. F. D. Moule, former professor of Divinity at Cambridge. He writes,

The Son's absolute and unique oneness with the Father is shown precisely in his submitting to the Father's will: "I and the Father are one" (x.30) precisely because "the Father is greater than I" (xiv.28). That is, Jesus exhibits the nature and character of God in the only way in which they can be absolutely and perfectly exhibited in the context of human behavior, namely in . . . a relationship . . . of glad and willing filial obedience. To this extent the paradox of . . . equality and subordination, is resolved in that relationship of perfect intimacy and identity of purpose which expresses itself in perfect obedience.

Moule, "The Manhood of Jesus in the New Testament," in *Christ, Faith and History: Cambridge Studies in Christology*, eds. Stephen W. Sykes and J. P. Clayton (Cambridge: Cambridge University Press, 1972), 101. In other words, if Jesus is God and therefore co-equal with the

authority. The conclusion becomes clear: Jesus had authority because he lived in submission to the Father; because he was entirely submitted to the Father, he exercised fully his Father's authority.

Jesus, fully submitted to his Father, exercised the Father's authority in the power of the Spirit

How can this two-part answer the Bible gives on Jesus's authority be brought together into an integrated whole? To do this we need to be clear about the nature of the incarnation. Christian tradition unambiguously affirms that the person of Jesus is fully God and fully human. The difficulty arises when we ask how Jesus can be fully human when he is also God. Is he some sort of creature or mutant who only appears human but in reality is superhuman? If that is the case, we do not have a real incarnation, only a theophany wherein God appears as a man in Jesus, but Jesus is not truly human.

The only way to get around this is to recognize that at the incarnation, God the Son subjects his powers to divine self-restraint. For uninitiated readers, the idea that God the Son places his divine powers under some form of self-limitation may sound strange, or even outrageous and heretical. But this is a well-established theological view espoused by evangelical scholars, such as J. I. Packer and Gerald F. Hawthorne, built on the work of other earlier writers.

Packer in his book *Knowing God* was responding to the view that Jesus displays human limitations at times, such as not knowing certain things (e.g. Mark 5:30; 6:38; 13:32), because the incarnation process required him to renounce some of his divine attributes or powers in order for him to be fully human.[12] He rejects this because it makes God who is immutable or unchanging into one who can change simply by giving up some of his attributes, as if divine attributes are like our clothes, which we humans can change at will. Such a view of the incarnation actually violates the very being of God who is immutable, that is unchanging in his very nature. Packer goes on, instead, to provide a better explanation of how it is that Jesus at times displays divine powers and at other times seems bereft of them.

Father, what would be his relationship with God the Father in his incarnated state? The answer must be that, because he is sinless and perfect as a man, he would be the perfectly filial Son of his Father, living in total obedience to him. Thus the seeming paradox of equality with the Father and submission to him at one and the same time is fully reconciled.

12. This is the radical kenosis theory advanced by Bishop Charles Gore and others in the nineteenth century. See J. I. Packer, *Knowing God* (London: Hodder & Stoughton, 1973), 50–55 for an introduction.

It is true that Jesus' knowledge of things both human and divine are sometimes limited . . . The impression of Jesus which the gospels give is not that He was wholly bereft of divine knowledge and power, but that He drew on both intermittently, while being content for much of the time not to do so. The impression, in other words, is not so much one of deity reduced as of *divine capacities restrained* . . . How are we to account for this restraint? Surely in terms of the truth of which John's gospel in particular makes so much, the entire submission of the Son to the Father's will . . . The God-man did not know independently, any more than He acted independently. Just as He did not do all that He could have done, because certain things were not His Father's will (see Matt 26:53f), so He did not consciously know all that He might have known, but only what the Father willed Him to know. His knowing, like the rest of His activity, was bounded by His Father's will.[13]

Similarly, Gerald F. Hawthorne in his book *The Presence and the Power* argues that the thrust of New Testament teachings shows that Jesus exercised self-limitation over his divine powers in order to be truly human. He says that

to make this self-limitation possible, it is necessary to assume that . . . the Son, in obedience to the Father, made a conscious decision to set aside everything that would be incompatible with his ministry of humiliation and redemption. . . . Such an understanding of the person of Christ presupposes that the divine attributes of omniscience, omnipotence, and omnipresence are potential and latent during the Son's earthly life – present but not operative.[14]

In other words, for the purpose of the incarnation, the divine Son humbled himself (Phil 2:6–8) and subjected his divine powers of omnipotence, omniscience, and omnipresence fully to self-restraint. Only through the exercise of such a divine self-restraint could he be truly human. We may then ask: How is such a self-restraint or self-limitation possible for the divine Son? Would that not make him less than divine? The answer is that because the Son is divine, he is Lord of all power, knowledge, and space-time. Thus he has the perfect freedom to choose to exercise these powers or not to exercise them, without at any point diminishing his divinity, and this he does always in perfect

---

13. Packer, *Knowing God*, 54–55, emphasis added.
14. Gerald F. Hawthorne, *The Presence and the Power* (Dallas, TX: Word, 1991), 210–11.

harmony with his Father's will.[15] The point that both Packer and Hawthorne make in their respective quotations is fully consistent with what was asserted earlier, which is that Jesus's authority flows out of his submission to the Father.

We can now bring the various threads together. Most of the time when we think of the incarnation we think of the concept of "the Word [becoming] flesh" (John 1:14) primarily as Jesus the Son taking on flesh, with little or no reference to his Trinitarian relationship with the Father and the Spirit. However, when we bring together what we have examined above concerning Jesus's relationship to his Father and to the Holy Spirit we find ourselves arriving at a much deeper Trinitarian understanding of the incarnation instead. Jesus conceived by the Holy Spirit took on flesh. In his earthly life, he lived in total submission to the Father and, as the perfectly filial Son, did only what his Father willed him to do. Thus in all that he did he was exercising his Father's authority in the power of the Holy Spirit acting through his humanity.[16]

When the incarnation is understood in this manner, it can be seen that Jesus modelled for us what God also willed for all humans who are redeemed in Christ. As Jesus was conceived by the Holy Spirit (Matt 1:18–20; Luke 1:35), we too must be born again of the Spirit (John 3:3–8). As Jesus was empowered through the coming of the Spirit upon him at his baptism (Matt 3:16; Mark 1:10; Luke 3:21–22; 4:1; John 1:32), so we too are empowered through the baptism of the Spirit (Matt 3:11; Luke 3:16; John 1:33; Acts 1:5; 11:16; 1 Cor 12:13).[17] As Jesus's authority rested fully on his submission to the Father, we too can exercise our heavenly Father's authority in the power of the Spirit to the extent we are yielded to God.[18]

---

15. We see this illustrated in Jesus's exercise of his omnipresence as the divine Son. Omnipresence does not mean that the divine Son is necessarily bound to be everywhere in space-time but rather that he is the Lord of space-time. Thus for his incarnation, he wills not to be everywhere but to limit himself to be located at a particular point in space-time, and this he can freely do without diminishing his divinity in any way. The same argument applies for his omnipotence and omniscience.

16. Hawthorne actually goes beyond Packer in his integration of the work of the Holy Spirit in the life and ministry of Jesus. Packer speaks of Jesus's entire submission to the Father, and acting and knowing what his Father willed him to do and know, but without specific reference to the role of the Spirit. Hawthorne goes further to state "that Jesus was truly dependent upon the Holy Spirit, not for permission to use his own power, but for the very power itself with which he did his mighty works" (Hawthorne, *Presence and the Power*, 218). Footnote 18, below, draws attention to the same point being made by Thomas A. Smail.

17. Here I am simply referring to the "baptism of/with the Spirit" as taught in the New Testament without going into the alternative interpretations of the phrase.

18. On this subject of Jesus's authority and the Christian's authority as stated in John 14:12, apart from Hawthorne (*Presence and the Power,* esp. 199–244), I would also refer the reader to Thomas A. Smail who succinctly sums up the issue as follows:

This is exactly what Jesus means when he said, "Truly, truly, I say to you, whoever believes in me will also do the works that I do; and greater works than these will he do, because I am going to the Father" (John 14:12). The key to this verse is what the last clause "because I am going to the Father" refers to. The context is the Upper Room Discourse wherein Jesus is preparing his disciples for his impending death. He then goes on to inform them that when he returns to the Father, he will send the Holy Spirit to them (John 14:15–31; 15:26–16:15). Indeed he promises his disciples, "And I will ask the Father, and he will give you another Helper, to be with you forever, even the Spirit of Truth" (14:16–17). He further explains that "it is to your advantage that I go away, for if I do not go away, the Helper will not come to you. But if I go, I will send him to you" (16:7). Thus we can only fully grasp what Jesus means in John 14:12 when we link it to the promised coming of the Holy Spirit after the death, resurrection, and ascension of Jesus.

This also helps us to understand what Jesus means by "greater works than these will he do." Because whatever Jesus's disciples can do is being done through the power of the same Spirit who empowered the incarnate Jesus, the "greater works" can only refer to what is quantitatively, not qualitatively, greater. As Archbishop William Temple puts it, "In scale, if not in quality, the works of Christ, wrought through His disciples are greater than those wrought by Him in His earthly ministry."[19] Thus, for example, Billy Graham is indeed one of the most renowned evangelists of the twentieth century, having brought to faith many times more the number reached by our Lord Jesus himself. Nevertheless, his evangelistic work is only quantitatively, never qualitatively, greater than Christ's.

The Heart of Spiritual Authority

We began by asking the question of how a person with the fundamental disposition of a servant can have the authority in ministry to change lives and

---

Christ's explicit statement in John 14:12 is quite decisively to the effect that he who is joined to him by faith shall do the works that he did, that everything that was possible to him is possible to his people; that therefore his power does not rest solely and exclusively in his divinity, but is conferred upon his humanity. He always acts, not only as God Incarnate, but throughout as a man anointed and full of the Holy Spirit, and what by the Spirit he does in his own human nature is the basis and promise of what he will do in ours.

Thomas A. Smail, *Reflected Glory: The Spirit in Christ and Christians* (London: Hodder & Stoughton, 1975), 69.

19. William Temple, *Readings in St. John's Gospel* (London: Macmillan, 1950), 235.

the world. We noted that those in leadership usually have at their disposal two kinds of authority. The first is the institutional authority of the office they hold, which gives them executive power that is clearly defined and concrete. The second is the personal moral authority, which is linked to a person's character, integrity, moral standing in community, and ability to inspire a following. It is much less tangible but can be easily discerned by the thoughtful and observant. Although the first often gives position, status, and authority to command obedience, clearly it is the second that is much more crucial in leadership. Those who seek to exercise institutional executive powers without the undergirding of personal moral authority often lose the respect of those under them. Conversely those who have personal moral authority often impact the lives of others without the need of strong institutional authority.

But we have argued further that over and above these two kinds of authority there is a third kind of authority in the Christian life that we refer to as spiritual authority. This kind of authority does not act necessarily independently of the first two kinds, but usually acts in tandem with them and, at the same time, over and above them. We see this repeatedly in the lives of those who have been used greatly by God in the church. And we see this as supremely manifested in the life of Jesus, the God who lived as a full-blooded human. What then is the source of Jesus's authority and where did the power of his ministry come from?

The clear answer from the Bible is that the power in his ministry came through the empowering of the Holy Spirit, which was poured out upon him at his baptism. But that is not something that is independent of his relationship to his Father who sent him for the salvation on the world. As John has pointed out explicitly, Jesus the Son can do nothing of his own accord. As the perfect Son he does only what the Father wills, and when he does what the Father commands, he exercises the full authority of the Father in the Spirit's power. Precisely because he says that "the Son can do nothing of his own accord" (John 5:19), he therefore could also say "All authority in heaven and earth has been given to me" (Matt 28:18).

Pentecostal-charismatic writers and others are right when they point out that the authority of Jesus comes through the anointing of the Holy Spirit who came upon him in power at his baptism. But what these writers often fail to emphasize is the complete obedience of the Son to his Father's will, without which there would have been no incarnation in the first place and all that flows from it. Thus, ultimately, it must be asserted that the heart of Jesus's authority is rooted in his total submission to the Father. In the next chapter we will expand on this in more detail.

4

Submission as the Path to Authority

In the previous chapter I have argued that the source of Jesus's authority in his earthly ministry is found in his total submission to the Father. This conclusion was reached after a careful examination of what the Gospels in particular tell us about the incarnate Christ. In his unambiguous statement in John 14:12, our Lord informs us that his own modus operandi in his incarnated state is also the model for us. Thus just as his spiritual authority is rooted in his obedience to the Father, in the same way we will have authority to the extent that we are yielded to the Father. Just as he exercised his Father's authority in the power of the Holy Spirit, similarly we through the power of the Holy Spirit can exercise the Father's authority.

The idea or principle that the path to spiritual authority lies in submission goes against almost everything that this world stands for. Here is found one of the greatest paradoxes of the Christian life. What is taught about authority in the New Testament is the exact opposite of the ways of this world. Mao Zedong, the first leader of Communist China summed up the world's wisdom neatly in his famous saying, "Political power grows out of the barrel of a gun"! Even if leaders in this world do not state it so baldly, they nonetheless practice the same through the use of naked executive power, threats and unsubtle arm-twisting, multifold forms of seduction, uncontrolled anger, put-downs for those perceived as threats, half-truths, fake news, and the like. The goal is to employ every weapon at our disposal to get what we want, often irrespective of moral considerations or human consequences.

Thus the submission principle is a paradox that needs further elaboration. We will look at four related issues here. First, apart from John's Gospel, which we looked at in the previous chapter, we will look at other evidence in the New

Testament that points to the same principle. Second, given that the principle of submission goes against the ways of the world we need to be sure that this alternative is rooted in sound Christian thinking. Third, we will go further to argue that in the work of the kingdom of God, only genuine spiritual authority derived from the Father ultimately matters. Last, we will look briefly at how the principle of submission is to be practiced.

Further Support for the Submission Principle in the New Testament

Are there other New Testament passages that support the assertion that Jesus's authority in his earthly ministry is rooted in his total submission to the Father? There are at least two clear examples that we will now turn to.

We begin with the temptation narratives of Jesus (Luke 4:1–13; see also Matt 4:1–11). Various interpretations have been given as to the nature of the three temptations that the devil puts before him. Thomas Smail, a Scottish theologian and former director of Fountain Trust, and others have suggested that the temptations are related directly to Jesus's baptism, where he received his Father's clear affirmation, "You are my beloved Son; with you I am well pleased" (Luke 3:22; see also Matt 3:17) and his empowering by the Spirit. Hence the devil's repeated words "If you are the son of God . . ." (Luke 4:3, 9; see also Matt 4:3, 6) are aimed at making Jesus entertain doubts over his relationship with the Father. The first temptation is to make him "*presume* on his Sonship" by using the Spirit's power for self-gratification of his hunger through turning stone into bread. The second tempts him to "*abandon* his Sonship" by worshipping the devil. The third seeks to entice him to "*prove* his Sonship" by jumping off the top of the temple, thus doing something spectacular and superhuman so as to draw the world to himself.[1] As Smail puts it,

> The whole thrust of his temptation, above and beyond its specific content, is to separate his employment of the Spirit's power from his status and vocation of Sonship. To use the power of the Spirit in a sanctified way is to use it as a Son, and the attack of the tempter is calculated to cast doubt in different ways upon his vocation as Son.[2]

We may or may not agree with the precise details of the above interpretation of Jesus's temptations. But what is absolutely clear is that in each case Jesus's

---

1. Smail, *Reflected Glory*, 90–95.
2. Smail, 92.

response begins with "it is written" or "it is said" (Luke 4:8, 10, and 12) and is then completed with an appropriate quotation from the Old Testament. Thus, whereas the devil tries his best to make Jesus doubt his Sonship, Jesus responds with a clear reaffirmation of his Sonship by quoting God's word in rebuttal. To put it another way, the devil knows where the heart of Jesus's authority in ministry lies and goes for the jugular. Jesus the Son responds in exactly the way that a perfectly filial Son should, which is to reaffirm his obedience to the Father through living by his word. By doing so, he not only throws out all doubts about his relationship to the Father, which the devil seeks to put into his head, but through calling on the Father's authority he defeats the devil instead.

The second clear example in the New Testament that links Jesus's authority to his submission to the Father is the christological hymn of Philippians 2:5–11.[3] Here Paul is addressing the issue of disunity in the church in Philippi (cf. Phil 2:1–4; 4:2–5) and urges the members there to avoid self-seeking ambition and pride by humbling themselves towards each other. He then urges upon them the example of our Lord:

> Have this mind among yourselves, which is yours in Christ Jesus, who, though he was in the form of God, did not count equality with God a thing to be grasped, but emptied himself, by taking the form of a servant, being born in the likeness of men. And being found in human form, he humbled himself by becoming obedient to the point of death, even death on a cross. Therefore God has highly exalted him and bestowed on him the name that is above every name, so that at the name of Jesus every knee should bow, in heaven and on earth and under the earth, and every tongue confess that Jesus Christ is Lord, to the glory of God the Father. (2:5–11)

What Paul is saying about Jesus is that, though "he was in the form of God, did not count equality with God a thing to be grasped," meaning that though he is God in himself, he refuses to hang on to his divine status and privilege. For the purpose of the incarnation he "emptied himself" of his divine glory (not his divine attributes or qualities), that is, not grasping tightly onto his divine status but letting go instead. Thus he takes the position and role of a lowly servant so as to be born human. In submission to the Father, he humbles himself all the way, from heaven to the cross. Because he humbles himself

---

3. Many scholars are in agreement that these verses almost certainly originated in an early christological hymn used in the New Testament church and quoted here by Paul.

without reserve, he is now highly exalted by his Father above everything "in heaven and on earth and under the earth."

All this is of a piece with what we have looked at in the previous three chapters on servanthood and submission. We have noted how Jesus firmly admonished his disciples that "If anyone would be first, he must be last of all and servant of all" (Mark 9:35). Furthermore, "whoever would be great among you must be your servant, and whoever would be first among you must be slave of all" (Mark 10:43–44). Similarly, here in Philippians Paul asserts that because Jesus "humbled himself by becoming obedient to the point of death," therefore God the Father has "highly exalted him and bestowed on him the name that is above every name" (Phil 2:8–9).

Just as the path of true spiritual greatness lies through humility and servanthood, so the path of genuine spiritual authority lies in submission to the Father. As noted earlier, precisely because Jesus of his own free will could say that "the Son can do nothing of his own accord" (John 5:19), he could also assert that "All authority in heaven and on earth has been given to me" (Matt 28:18)! You cannot have the latter without the former.

Submission versus the Present *Zeitgeist*

Submission has never been a popular word in human history. Human rebellion against God and his laws began in Eden. Paul's conclusion that "all have sinned and fall short of the glory of God" (Rom 3:23) informs us how pervasive it is to this very day. This rebellion has now come to be enshrined in our modern and postmodern worldviews where autonomous freedom and self-evident human rights are often glorified to the exclusion of human and social responsibilities. That is our present *Zeitgeist*, the spirit of our age.

Within this *Zeitgeist* there is a general revulsion against all forms of external authority that is further fueled by modern psychology's teachings on self-actualization and self-realization. Paul Vitz, Professor Emeritus of Psychology at New York University, in his book *Psychology as Religion* lists the major self-theorists behind this movement as Carl Jung, Erich Fromm, Carl Rogers, Abraham Maslow, and Rollo May.[4] The central concern of their respective versions of humanistic "selfist psychology" is about fulfilling one's full potential as a human being. It was this trend that Vitz sees as paving the way for what he terms as the utter "selfism" of society.

---

4. Paul C. Vitz, *Psychology as Religion: The Cult of Self-Worship*, 2nd ed. (Grand Rapids, MI: Eerdmans, 1994), 1–14.

The emphasis on fulfilling one's fullest potential within appropriate God-given limits and allowing others to do the same is an important Christian idea. This needs to be properly affirmed, but it is very different from the self-actualization concept of today's selfist psychology, which clearly has a sinister side. Unlike the Christian view of human nature as sinful, selfism is built on a belief in "the complete goodness of human nature."[5] No wonder the psychiatrist and pastor John White, in his book *The Shattered Mirror*, critiques it as follows:

> If I am interested primarily in me, if I have an undeniable right to realize my full potential – then logically my neighbors must take second place. My needs will take precedence over theirs whenever the two conflict. I would be loath to admit this. But logically it follows. The other person is devalued. I am number one . . . While the "virtue" of me-first-ism was not acclaimed by the movement as a whole, the expression certainly represents a logical conclusion from its most basic tenet – I have the right to realize my full potential as a human being, in sexual practices, in my ambitions and in every other way. This philosophy ends up deifying the individual.[6]

White's point is plain. Self-actualization as taught by selfist psychologists makes me the center of my life. Everyone else becomes secondary at best. Moreover there are no restraints on me. The end of the matter inevitably is to make myself my own god, hence the subtitle of Vitz's book is *The Cult of Self-Worship*. Within such a worldview there can be no meaningful talk of submission to another.

We need to come back to sound biblical thinking here. Whereas selfist psychologists emphasize self-actualization, the Bible speaks instead about "dying to self" using a variety of metaphors (cf. Luke 9:23, 24; John 12:24–26; Rom 6:6; 8:13; Col 3:5; etc.). Because of the pervasiveness of human corruption (Jer 17:9) and the universality of sin (Rom 3:23), our sinful nature has left us in bondage to sin and its power (Rom 7:15–20). Without the grace of God, self-actualization can only lead to the actualization of our sinful humanity.

This understanding of human nature is summed up neatly by Martin Luther in the title of probably his most important book, *The Bondage of the*

---

5. Vitz, *Psychology as Religion*, 140.

6. John White, *The Shattered Mirror: Reflections on Being Human* (Leicester: Inter-Varsity Press, 1987), 41.

Will.[7] In this, he was merely following in the footsteps of Augustine, who had defended the biblical understanding of sin and human bondage against Pelagius more than a thousand years before. Augustine affirms that humans do have free will, but that freedom has been weakened and incapacitated by sin, although not completely lost. We are therefore unable to freely turn to God and to choose good unless our free will is restored and empowered through the work of God's grace. He sums this up in his *Confessions*, in the context of the discussion on sexual purity, with the simple statement, "You command us to be continent; give what you command, and command what you will."[8]

To sum up, because of our sinful human nature, human will is free merely in the sense that, apart from God's help, it is free to sin. Only by the grace of God can the human will be enabled to turn Godward, choose what is right and obey his law. This is something that modern selfism does not and cannot understand because it is built on a completely different view of human nature, which is that it is completely good.

Towards the end of his critique, Vitz asserts that the proper response to selfist psychology's deification of the self is for the Christian to let go of the self and its controlling will. "It is precisely for this reason that the New Testament is so thoroughly characterized by motives and metaphors that are directly antithetical to the psychology of the independent, autonomous, rebellious, self-created-self."[9] This is essentially the same as what we have referred to above as dying to self. He then goes on to speak of the need for Christians today to be re-educated "on radical obedience, on the mysticism of submissive surrender of the will, on the beauty of dependency, on how to find humility."[10] We should note that each of the four qualities that Vitz here urges upon Christians today is part and parcel of what submission to God entails.

At the beginning of this section we noted that the spirit of our age has largely been defined by autonomy and self-evident human rights, often magnified in popular thinking to the exclusion of human and social responsibilities. Clearly the selfist concept of self-actualization is part and parcel of this *Zeitgeist*.

---

7. Martin Luther, *The Bondage of the Will*, trans. J. I. Packer and O. R. Johnston (Cambridge: James Clarke, 1957). This was Luther's rebuttal of Erasmus, the most accomplished classical scholar of his day, in his defense of Pelagius's argument for the complete freedom of the human will.

8. Augustine, *The Confessions*, book 10.29.40, trans. and ed. by Philip Burton (New York, NY: Knopf, 2001), 240. For a neat summary of Augustine's position and his controversy with Pelagius, see Alister E. McGrath, *Christian Theology: An Introduction*, 6th ed. (Oxford: Wiley-Blackwell, 2017), 330–34.

9. Vitz, *Psychology as Religion*, 160.

10. Vitz, 162.

Various voices have been raised against the autonomous and unrestraint freedom now being advocated and widely practiced in the modern world, especially in the West.

One such voice is that of the late Aleksandr Solzhenitsyn, Nobel laureate and famous Russian dissident of the Soviet era. In his 1978 Harvard Commencement address he offered a sharp critique of the rampant practice of some in the West who assert their freedom to the point that, in his perception, it becomes socially harmful and destructive. Solzhenitsyn contends:

> The defense of individual rights has reached such extremes as to make society as a whole defenseless against certain individuals. It is time, in the West, to defend not so much human rights as human obligations. . . . Destructive and irresponsible freedom has been granted boundless space. Society appears to have little defense against the abyss of human decadence.[11]

For the Christian, the principle of submission modelled by Jesus is the perfect antidote to the self-assertion and autonomous freedom of the spirit of our age. In him we see a man who lives a life of total obedience to the Father and yet is perfectly free in himself, living responsibly in the context of his time, and always engaging others with confidence and love. He invites us to travel the same road with him.

In the Work of the Kingdom of God, Only Genuine Spiritual Authority Matters

In the previous chapter, we looked at the nature of authority in the ministry of the church and mission. We noted that three kinds of authority are at play. The first is the institutional and executive authority that comes with position and office. The second is the personal and moral authority that a person possesses by virtue of their life, character, and maturity. Over and above these two is a third kind that we have termed spiritual authority, which comes through the empowering of the Holy Spirit.

Although this spiritual authority often functions in tandem with the first two, especially the second, nevertheless at times it manifests itself in ways that are totally out of proportion to what the first two kinds of authority can

---

11. Aleksandr Solzhenitsyn, "A World Split apart," Harvard Commencement Address, 8 June, 1978, *American Rhetoric*, https://www.americanrhetoric.com/speeches/alexandersolzhenitsynharvard.htm.

accomplish. Moreover, what we also find is that this authority is given by God to his servants often regardless of human factors such as education or training, intellectual prowess or institutional backing, ethnicity, social class, and the like. This is what we find when we examine the lives of those mentioned in the last chapter.

Among the apostles, we see demonstrations of great power in evangelistic breakthroughs, and in signs and wonders in Peter's ministry in Acts 2 and elsewhere in the New Testament. We also find the same in Paul's missionary work. Yet one was a mere fisherman by trade, the other an outstanding rabbinic scholar. In the twentieth century we see the same pattern in the amazing ministries of Prophet Harris in West Africa on the one hand and John Sung among the Chinese churches on the other. Harris had an average education, but Sung was a brilliant scholar with an American PhD. Here again their different backgrounds seem to matter little, with the Spirit's anointing making human endowments and training irrelevant. In the case of Pope John Paul II and John Stott, both were great intellects and highly trained. But the Pope had the full weight of the papal office and the Catholic church behind him, while Stott had almost no comparable institutional backing. Yet both their ministries had global impact. All these people exercised an authority that appears to have come from beyond themselves. In their lives and ministries, clearly there were times when the powers of heaven touched earth to bring us into the presence of God.

But there is more. Jesus, in his parting instructions to his disciples, makes it very clear that in the work of the kingdom, only genuine spiritual authority matters. In Matthew's account, he tells the disciples just before his ascension that "All authority in heaven and on earth has been given to me. Go therefore and make disciples of all nations . . ." (Matt 28:18–19). The "therefore" in verse 19 clearly implies that Jesus is instructing the disciples to take the authority that the Father had given to him, and with that authority to go and "make disciples of all nations." Without such authority, which comes only from the Holy Spirit through the risen Christ, the church will get nowhere in the battle for the kingdom. Hence in Luke's account, Jesus did not just promise the endowment of power through the Spirit in Acts 1:8, he explicitly instructed the disciples "to wait for the promise of the Father" (Acts 1:4) before fanning out in mission to the nations.

One final point needs noting. In the previous chapter we argued that the authority of Jesus rested on his submission to the Father and was simultaneously exercised through the power of the Spirit. In the same way, just as we have been called to exercise spiritual authority in the power of the Holy Spirit, the authority we exercise must also ultimately be rooted in our submission to the Father. Without that submission or obedience, there can be no genuine spiritual authority in our lives and ministries. A careful study of the lives of those who have exercised such authority will again and again demonstrate that the submission principle is paramount. We will briefly look at three examples here.

We begin with Martin Luther, the acknowledged leader of the sixteenth-century Reformation. In 1521, at the height of the Reformation battles, he was summoned to appear before the emperor, the princes, and church authorities, to answer charges of heresy. As the trial drew to a climactic end, he was asked to recant his views and repudiate all the errors in his books. Luther was in an extremely vulnerable position and knew that, despite the safe conduct pass from the emperor, he could be seized and burnt at the stake. But his courageous and ringing response will forever remain one of the classic statements of church history:

> Unless I am convicted by Scriptures and plain reason – I do not accept the authority of popes and councils, for they have contradicted each other – my conscience is captive to the Word of God. I cannot and I will not recant anything, for to go against conscience is neither right nor safe. (Here I stand. I can do no other.) God help me. Amen.[12]

Luther effectively did exactly the same as his Master, Jesus Christ, who responded to the devil at his temptation by quoting from the Scriptures. His submission to Scriptures, even at the risk of his own life, was the basis of his spiritual authority as the leading figure of the Reformation. It opened the way not only for the reform of Christianity but also for a powerful spiritual revival that swept through Europe, fundamentally reshaping it in the process.

Something similar is seen in the life of George Whitefield, widely regarded as the greatest evangelist of the eighteenth-century revival on both sides of the Atlantic. Shortly after his conversion in Oxford he wrote in his journal, "I began to read the Holy Scripture upon my knees laying aside all other books, and praying over, if possible, every line and word. This proved meat indeed and drink indeed to my soul. I daily received fresh life, light and power from

---

12. Cited in Roland H. Bainton, *Here I Stand: A Life of Martin Luther* (New York: Abingdon, 1950), 144. Although there is some uncertainty whether Luther actually uttered the words in brackets, Bainton thinks that they are genuine.

above."[13] Whitefield, as is widely known, already possessed remarkable natural gifts as an orator. Yet the power of his preaching rested not on those gifts, but rather, as it appears, on his self-humbling before God and submission to his word.

We finally turn to a quite different illustration of the principle of submission in the life of a man called Simon Kimbangu (1889–1951) from Congo.[14] Kimbangu had only very basic education and worked for a few years as a teacher and an evangelist. In the midst of the worldwide flu pandemic of 1918 he received his first call. He heard a voice saying, "I am Christ, my servants are unfaithful. I have chosen you to bear witness before your brethren and to convert them. Tend my flock."[15] Kimbangu resisted the call for three years and even tried to run away from his base in Nkamba, despite God's voice coming to him night after night. Finally on 6 April 1921 he responded, and his ministry brought great numbers to faith. Many were healed and a few even brought back to life from death. The success of the revival aroused opposition from two groups. The colonial Belgian planters were unhappy because their plantation workers were running off to the revival meetings. The western missionaries were also upset, especially the Catholics, because they were losing members to the revival.

Three months after he began his ministry he went into hiding because the Belgian colonial authorities were seeking his arrest. But after another three months, Kimbangu heard God's voice again, "Return to Nkamba to be arrested."[16] He obeyed in spite of his followers' protests and was arrested immediately on 12 September 1921. He was charged with fomenting rebellion and sentenced to death, plus a hundred and twenty lashes. The death penalty was commuted to life sentence only at the intervention of American Baptist missionaries and he was sent off to prison thousands of kilometers from home. Though an exemplary prisoner he was never released, and died in prison after thirty years.

---

13. *George Whitefield's Journals*, first published between 1738 and 1741 (Edinburgh: Banner of Truth, 1960), 60; cited in John R. W. Stott, *Understanding the Bible*, rev. ed. (Milton Keynes: Scripture Union, 1984), 168.

14. See Marie-Louise Martin, *Kimbangu: An African Prophet and His Church* (Oxford: Blackwell, 1975). See also the various articles by different scholars on "Simon Kimbangu" in the *Dictionary of African Christian Biography*, ed. Jonathan J. Bonk, et. al. (1998, with regular updating), https://dacb.org/ (accessed 2 November 2020).

15. Cited in Martin, *Kimbangu*, 44.

16. Martin, 60.

But what is most important for our study on submission is what happened subsequently. The Kimbanguist Church that sprung up became the largest indigenous Christian movement in all of Africa and was the first African Indigenous Church to be received into the membership of the World Council of Churches in 1969. The *World Christian Encyclopedia*[17] records that, as of 2015, it has 16,000 congregations and some 6,439,000 adult members in the Democratic Republic of Congo alone. Not bad for six months of preaching! But would the story have been the same had Kimbangu not submitted to God's voice to give himself up, allowed himself to be unjustly and cruelly flogged, and thrown into prison for thirty years until his death? God's ways are strange, aren't they? Perhaps . . .

Submission in Practice

If the principle of submission is so fundamental to Christian life and ministry how does it work out in practice? Some significant examples have already been given above. We will now elaborate further.

To Whom or What Are We To Submit

We begin with the question to whom and what are we called to submit?

God's word

For Christians who take the Bible as our primary source of authority in all matters of faith and conduct, the first answer must be God's word in the Scriptures. Never accept a word that goes against the plain teaching of Scripture. This may be a well-worn theme for many of us but, because it is so fundamental, some things are worth repeating. Years ago, as a university student, I heard the wise words of a preacher who urged us to avoid the two errors committed respectively by the Pharisees and Sadducees of Jesus's days. The former added to the Bible by multiplying the laws of God; the latter took away from the Bible by denying many of its truths such as life after death. The Cape Town Commitment issued by the Third Lausanne Conference on World Evangelization, 2010, has some important things to say about both these errors.

Against the danger of Pharisaism, it states, "We affirm that the Bible is the final written word of God, not surpassed by any further revelation, but we also

---

17. Todd M. Johnston and Gina A. Zurlo, eds., *World Christian Encyclopedia*, 3rd ed. (Edinburgh: University of Edinburgh Press, 2020), 219.

rejoice that the Holy Spirit illumines the minds of God's people so that the Bible continues to speak God's truth in fresh ways to people in every culture."[18] The statement clearly affirms that the Holy Spirit continues to work in all cultures through the Bible to bring new light and speak in fresh ways. At the same time, it does so without compromising the finality of God's revelation in the Bible, affirming that nothing new can be put on a par with it as revelation.

Against the tendency to take away from God's word like the Sadducees, The Cape Town Commitment categorically states,

> We live however, in a world full of lies and rejection of the truth. Many cultures display a dominant relativism that denies that any absolute truth exists or can be known. If we love the Bible, then we must rise to the defense of its truth claims. We must find fresh ways to articulate biblical authority in all cultures.[19]

It is a clarion call to all Christians to stand firm on its authority and to defend its truth claims.

God's voice through conscience, prayer, inner conviction, the prophetic word, and his clear leading otherwise

But God does not only speak to us through his objective word in the Bible. Christians have always affirmed that he also speaks to us through his subjective work and voice in our spirit, heart, and mind. This happens, for example, when Whitefield prays and meditates on God's word on his knees, or when God instructs Kimbangu to give himself up to the colonial authorities. We need to learn to listen to God. Jesus clearly says that his sheep recognize his voice. "I know my own and my own know me" (John 10:14).

Space does not allow for a fuller discussion here, but two brief comments seem appropriate. First, it does appear that most Christians nowadays have lost the art of hearing God. This is something that the church today is in desperate need of recovering. Second, in this exercise, one should always remember that God's subjective leading never takes us beyond the boundaries laid down in his objective word, the Bible. Strict observance of this principle will prevent us from falling foolishly into heresy and moral disaster.

---

18. Lausanne Movement, "The Cape Town Commitment: A Confession of Faith and a Call to Action," (2010), Part 1, paragraph 6, https://www.lausanne.org/content/ctcommitment#p1-6.

19. Lausanne Movement, "Cape Town Commitment."

To those whom God places over us

It is easier to speak of submitting to God than to speak of submitting to those who are above us in the line of authority, whether in church or in Christian ministry. The Bible speaks of submitting to those over us (e.g. 1 Cor 16:16; Heb 13:17) as well as submitting to one another within the fellowship of the church (e.g. Eph 5:21). But many of us have heard the refrain, "I will submit to God but why should I submit to you?" directed against someone in authority. This is a widespread problem all over, and within Protestant churches in particular, with many leaders claiming to have a direct hotline to heaven. Thus the problem of myriads of splintered and independent churches has become one of the major sources of Christian disunity in the world.

On this issue of submitting to those above us, it is helpful to be reminded of the episode when Jesus was left behind in the temple at the age of twelve (Luke 2:41–52). The reactions of the rabbinic teachers to his questions and answers, together with the subsequent conversation with his parents after they found him, clearly indicate that his spiritual understanding by then had already surpassed that of his own earthly parents. Yet Luke's account goes on to tell us that Jesus "went down with them and came to Nazareth and was submissive to them" (v.51). For the incarnate Son, submission to his heavenly Father included submitting to his earthly parents whom the Father had placed over him.

But how far does our submission to human authorities go? Again, this is too big an issue to be discussed in detail here. But Richard Foster in his book *Celebration of Discipline* sums up his position with this statement, "Revolutionary submission commands us to live in submission to human authority until it becomes destructive."[20] In principle that would be a good place to draw the line, but applying it in actual situations, as for example in Simon Kimbangu's case, still requires careful spiritual discernment.

Submission and Servanthood as Inseparable

By now, I hope that you can see that you cannot separate servanthood and submission. Our Lord in Mark 10:43–44 calls us to servanthood: "But whoever would be great among you must be your servant, and whoever would be first among you must be slave of all." Then in the next breath he tells us that this too is how his earthly identity is defined: "For even the Son of Man came not to be served but to serve, and to give his life as a ransom for many" (v.45). But

---

20. Richard Foster, *Celebration of Discipline: The Path to Spiritual Growth*, 3rd ed. (New York: Harper San Francisco, 1998), 124.

for that identity as a servant to be lived out, it had to begin in his self-humbling in submission to his Father (Phil 2:6–8), without which there would have been no incarnation in the first place.

All that we have discussed in these four chapters revolves around these two inseparable themes. You cannot have one without the other. Only those who have heard and clearly understood Jesus's call to servanthood will strive for the submission that alone can enable them to become true servants. Only those who have grasped the power of submission will know the fullness of the joy and blessing of true servanthood.

Submission – the Condition for Long-Term Growth in Spiritual Authority

In discussing spiritual authority, one of the most puzzling issues that confronts us is that there appear to be exceptions like Balaam in the book of Numbers and Samson in the book of Judges that do not seem to fit the rules. We are not referring to direct involvement with occult power and witchcraft as such, but rather with God's people going badly wrong.

Careful examination of the Balaam story (Num 22–24) shows that Balaam is not a pagan prophet or shaman but rather one of God's prophets gone rogue. No pagan prophet or shaman can say what he repeatedly told Balak and his messengers, "Though Balak were to give me his house full of silver or gold, I could not go beyond the command of the LORD my God to do less or more" (Num 22:18; 23:12). Yet in spite of the fact that he has become unfaithful through desire for personal gain, he remains a man with real prophetic gifting. The same is true of Samson who was blessed with supernatural physical strength by the Spirit of God (Judg 13:25; 14:6; etc.). Despite his sleeping around with Philistine women, God did not withdraw his anointing of power. The question that naturally comes to mind is why does God not take away his gifts from both men when their lives go so badly out of line?

The Bible does not give us straightforward answers on this. But part of the answer is found in Paul's comment as he wrestles with the question of why God has not rejected Israel as his chosen people, despite their repeated failure to keep their covenant with him. As he reflected on God's mysterious purposes, he concluded, "For the gifts and the calling of God are *irrevocable*" (Rom 11:29). The word "irrevocable" here is something none of us fully understands. Nevertheless, there is something more that we need to remember. If God were to withdraw all his gifts and endowments from his servants who do wrong, which of us would be left standing untouched? So the more important question we should ponder on is how much more could God have used Balaam had he not been overtaken by greed or Samson if he had learned self-control and given up his philandering?

For those of us in ministry and seeking to serve God, the question we must ask is how are we to grow in the exercise of spiritual authority over the long haul? How can our spiritual stamina be sustained through the long weary years of ministry? The answer has to be found at the place where we began, which is submission. It is a lifelong process that must be sustained to the end, just as Jesus's obedience went all the way to the cross. And our submission must be sustained over the years through radical obedience, daily repentance and holy living, servanthood marked by genuine humility before God and others, and the lifelong study of God's word and practice of prayer.

It is here that many in the Pentecostal-charismatic movements that have emerged both in the West and from indigenous revival movements in various parts of the Majority World are making a major mistake. Their experience of the work of the Holy Spirit in their lives has often been so reinvigorating and overwhelming that they sometimes over-emphasize it in an exaggerated and unhealthy manner. Thus when it comes to the question of spiritual authority, there is a strong emphasis on the "anointing of the Spirit" in their teaching, which is right and proper. But too often this is done without the corresponding stress on repentance, radical obedience, and holy living.[21] Here lies a fundamental error that must be recognized as such, otherwise God's work of renewal in revivals simply cannot be sustained because the Spirit is grieved and leaves (Eph 4:30). Our natural tendency, like the rest of the world, is to crave the glory of the resurrection and the power of the Spirit at Pentecost without the pain and shame of Calvary and the cross! That will not do.

If the church worldwide, and especially the churches in the Majority World, is to see a powerful work of God sweeping across the nations in our generation, we have no alternatives but to return to first things and not go for illicit and fruitless shortcuts. The path to true spiritual authority and of being sustained through the long, tiring, and sometimes tiresome, years of ministry in the exercise of God's awesome power must go through lifelong servanthood and submission. Nothing less will do.

---

21. I would like to stress that the renewal movements over the past 100 years or so have brought tremendous growth and blessings throughout the global church, especially in the Majority World, and that not all in these movements are guilty of the unhealthy and lopsided teaching on the "anointing of the Spirit" referred to here. However, I believe the problem is endemic in two sections of the global renewal movements. The first is among those indigenous churches in the Majority World where the Bible's teachings have not been fully understood and taught. The second is more serious and originates from Pentecostal-charismatic preachers in the West, especially the USA, and has been disseminated across the globe through their various versions of the prosperity gospel and their preoccupation with worldly success.

5

You Are My Beloved Child

In an address to some five hundred theological students in the USA many years ago, Bishop Stephen Neill made the following remarks in relation to ambition in ministry:

> For the Christian there is one place and only one place – the lowest place. That is the command of the Lord, and it is binding upon us all. As you enter on the work of ministry you must seek the place of hardest work, greatest sacrifice and least recognition, and there you must be content . . . If when you are toiling contentedly in the lower place those who have the authority to call men to special spheres in the Lord's vineyard come to you and say, "Friend, come up higher; this place of great eminence and heavier responsibility is the one in which you can now best serve," you may accept the call without fear and without anxiety; but never, never, never, if you have yourself desired or sought what is called advancement in the church.[1]

Neill's remarks illustrate neatly the case I have sought to make in the preceding chapters. In the first two chapters I argued that our call to ministry in God's kingdom is first and foremost to the task of a servant and not to that of a leader. In the next two chapters I further argued that the New Testament evidence points to Jesus's total submission to his Father as the ultimate source of his authority in his incarnate life. Precisely because he lived in total obedience to the Father, he was able to exercise fully his Father's authority. This modus operandi in the life of Christ is also meant to be the model for our life and ministry. For us to know this divine authority we too must learn to live in submission to God our Father.

---

1. Stephen Neill, *On the Ministry* (London: SCM, 1952), 41–42.

I am aware that this approach to ministry goes against much of what is presently being advocated and taught in the church. No doubt some readers are asking, Does all this make sense? Is this approach realistic? Some will argue that all this talk about submission to the Father will simply mean that others will just trample over us like doormats and shove us aside, when as leaders we should be taking charge and asserting our God-given authority for the advance of the gospel. Others may suggest that modern life is simply far too complex for vague and intangible concepts like servanthood and submission to God to be helpful, even if they are there in Scriptures. The task of world evangelization in our generation is huge and urgent, and to accomplish it firm leadership and concrete strategies are needed. No doubt there will be other objections as well.

It is not my intention to answer the specific objections raised above. Rather, allow me to respond briefly to the concerns raised as a whole. First, in the preceding chapters, I have simply tried to be faithful to the Bible, and the New Testament in particular. Second, I have further sought to illustrate the biblical principles enunciated with examples from church history and the lives of those who have gone before us, and to show how their ministries have contributed significantly to the advance of the gospel. Moreover, their example continues to speak powerfully to us today.

I am aware that the challenge is particularly acute for those of us who are younger, in the early years of ministry in church or mission, and raring to go. We have heard God's call to the ministry and are eager to make a difference for Christ. But from our youth we have been conditioned by our environment to think that to get anywhere we must assert ourselves in the way that the world demands. So to succeed in ministry, we must map out our career paths wisely by getting into the best schools, making sure that we have an impressive résumé, and interning with some big-name pastors, churches, or organizations. Only then will others take us seriously. That is the way the game is being played and, if we want to get anywhere, we must know the rules and have some ambition to succeed. Furthermore, we are often surrounded by coworkers, the older ones in particular, who are all caught up in the same scramble to succeed as leaders.

Given this scenario, Neill's counsel above appears to be custom-made for a life and career in Peter Pan's Never Land! That would be so if Neill himself had not been a prize-winning scholar at Cambridge, won a fellowship at Trinity College, led a distinguished missionary and academic career, and ended up writing the history of the Indian church on his own because "hardly anyone else but himself could handle all the fourteen languages necessary for the task."[2] With such exceptional gifts, would he not have had to resist the temptation of wanting to succeed fast? Would he not have had to overcome personal ambition through obedience, self-denial, and humble service? Where does all this leave us?

Given the above, the question before us is what will give a person the sense of security and confidence in their deepest convictions, spiritually and psychologically, to do things differently and to embrace the radical path of servanthood and submission in ministry? What would give us the deep-seated assurance that to follow the way of Christ is the right way forward when almost everything around us is telling us to go the other way? Sure, obedience to his command and being inspired by his example form part of the answer. But going against the tide is never easy. What would give us that inner strength that will sustain us in our obedience when the going gets real tough?

The answer has to be found in what it was that gave the incarnate Jesus himself the inner strength, as a fully human person, to keep going and persevere to the end in the path of servanthood and submission. The evidence in the Gospels shows that it was because he knew with absolute certainty that he was the Son of God, and that all that he did in obedience to his Father would find ultimate fulfillment within God's eternal purposes. Living in the security of his Father's love and protection, he did not need to entertain doubts about his ultimate destiny. His clear sense of identity gave him the absolute confidence needed to go all the way to Calvary – because come what may, that would not be the end! We will now look at this more closely.

Jesus the Son, Secure in His Father's Love

Earlier we had looked at John's account of the Last Supper on the night of Jesus's arrest. Not one of the disciples could bring himself to help get everyone ready for dinner by washing their dusty dirty feet. After all they had been arguing among themselves as to who among them was the greatest (Mark 9:34), and jockeying for the plum jobs in what they all thought would be the new cabinet when Jesus established his kingdom in Jerusalem (10:35–45). The disciples

---

2. Christopher Lamb, "Stephen Neill 1900–1984: Unafraid to Ask Ultimate Questions," in *Mission Legacies: Biographical Studies of Leaders of the Modern Missionary Movement*, eds. Gerald H. Anderson, Robert T. Coote, Norman A. Horner, and James M. Philipps (Maryknoll, NY: Orbis, 1994), 445–51, here p. 449.

showed themselves to be just another ambitious, competitive, and insecure bunch. None would want to appear inferior to the others in any way.

When I read John 13, I am often reminded of an incident in my high school days eons ago. It was a boys' school, but with some girls in the pre-university classes. Once a week there was an assembly for the whole school with the head teacher on a podium giving out the notices from written sheets held in his hand. Then one day the head teacher accidentally dropped the notices while addressing the school. The thousand boys froze, none daring to make a move, even though each knew the right thing to do. The suspense was finally broken when one of the older girls stepped forward and picked up the notices for the head teacher. Of course, the head teacher gave the boys a tongue lashing that day. But why did the boys fail to do what everyone knew was the right thing to do? Those who attended boys' schools will know the reason all too well. Any boy who had dared to pick up the notices for the head teacher would have been laughed at and mocked till the end of his school days, if not indeed his whole life, for currying favor with the head teacher. Like the disciples at the Last Supper, we boys were driven by our insecurities and the need to protect our self-image before our peers. Such fears and insecurities are played out endlessly throughout our lives.

Against this background of the disciples' human insecurity, John tells us that,

> Jesus, knowing that the Father had given all things into his hands, and that he had come from God and was going back to God, rose from supper. He laid aside his outer garments, and taking a towel, tied it around his waist. Then he poured water into a basin and began to wash the disciples' feet and to wipe them with the towel that was wrapped around him. (John 13:3–5)

Most expositors of this passage rightly draw attention to Jesus's self-humbling to perform a task that every one of his disciples deemed beneath his dignity. However, what is often missed and rarely gets more than a cursory mention is verse 3, "Jesus, knowing that the Father had given all things into his hands, and that he had come from God and was going back to God . . ." This verse sums up in a nutshell the secret behind Jesus's inner strength.

John, with profound insight into human life, identifies the three things in which the fundamental insecurities of our life are rooted. The first concerns who has the final say over my life and all that it involves. Is it me or someone I trust, or am I in the hands of some unknown or even malign force? The second concerns our fundamental identity. Who am I, what is my origin and do I belong? And the third question concerns my future. What lies before me in this life and what is my ultimate destiny? Because we are unsure of the answers to these basic questions for ourselves, many of us go through life deeply insecure as individuals.

John 13:3 is therefore crucial to our understanding of Jesus's inner life. To begin with, Jesus knows "that the Father had given all things into his hands," and that ultimately his Father is in control and not someone else. Thus when Peter takes out his sword and cuts the ear of the high priest's servant in an attempt to prevent his arrest, Jesus stops Peter with the words, "Do you think that I cannot appeal to my Father, and he will at once send me more than twelve legions of angels? But how then should the Scriptures be fulfilled, that it must be so?" (Matt 26:53–54). Similarly, he is not intimidated by Pilate who thinks that he has the final say over Jesus's life and death. Instead, with calm composure he tells Pilate, "You would have no authority over me at all unless it had been given you from above" (John 19:11). In these and other passages, Jesus demonstrates that he knows exactly who is in charge.

Second, John goes on to affirm that Jesus knows "that he had come from God," that is he knows his own origins and, therefore, his precise identity. Already, as a boy of twelve at the Jerusalem temple, his reply to his parents who searched for him for three days indicates that he is precociously conscious of his unique relationship with God. "Why were you looking for me? Did you not know that I must be in my Father's house?" (Luke 2:49). This clear sense of his identity is publicly affirmed at his baptism at Jordan through God's pronouncement "You are my beloved Son, with you I am well pleased" (Mark 1:11; cf. Matt 3:17; Luke 3:22), and reaffirmed at the transfiguration (Matt 17:5; Mark 9:7; Luke 9:35). Because he is absolutely clear about his identity as the Son, he therefore lives as the perfectly filial Son. Thus his submission to the Father flows out of the inner consciousness of his unique filial relationship with God.

Third, John goes on to state that Jesus knows that he is "going back to God," meaning that he is sure of his ultimate destiny. Even as he explains the true nature of his messiahship to his disciples, he reveals to them that his sacrifice on the cross is not the end of the story. As he begins his final journey to Jerusalem, he tells his disciples that "the Son of Man will be delivered over to the chief priests and the scribes, and they will condemn him to death and deliver him over to the Gentiles. And they will mock him and spit on him, and flog him and kill him. And after three days he will rise" (Mark 10:33–34). No doubt this is not the only time he speaks about his resurrection after death (cf. John 2:19–22; 11:25–27). But there is more. In the Upper Room Discourse

(John 14–17) during the Last Supper, he explicitly and repeatedly speaks of his eventual return to the Father (e.g. 14:1–4, 28; 16:5–7, 28), as well as his ongoing relationship with his disciples. Jesus knows exactly what his final destiny will be.

Thus we can see from John 13:3 that Jesus had no doubts about who was in control over his earthly life, that he was perfectly clear about his origins and his identity as the incarnate Son, and that he was confident that his ultimate destiny was absolutely safe in his Father's hands. I can still vividly remember Joyce Baldwin, one of my Old Testament teachers, preaching on this passage at the college chapel years ago. When she summed up the situation with the words "Jesus, secure in his Father's love . . ." it was like a brilliant shaft of light that gave me a whole new understanding of the inner life of the human Jesus and, by implication, a totally new perspective on the Christian life. Unfettered by his disciples' egomania and wounded self-esteem as they sought to assert themselves all around him, Jesus, secure in his Father's love, took up the servant's towel.

But that is not all. In that final scene at Gethsemane just before his arrest, we find Jesus wrestling in prayer with his Father one last time, if possible to find a way to avert, not so much the physical suffering and the public humiliation of the cross, but the spiritually infinite pain of taking upon himself the wrath of God against sin. Yet even at that hour of decision, precisely because Jesus knows "that the Father had given all things into his hands, and that he had come from God and was going back to God," he could yield himself fully with the words, "Abba, Father . . . Yet not what I will, but what you will" (Mark 14:36; cf. Matt 26:39, 42; Luke 22:42). The incarnate Jesus submits himself to the Father's will to the very end because he lives every moment secure in his Father's love.

How then can we appropriate what we see in the life of the human Jesus and learn to live in the same manner?

New Testament Teachings on God as our Father

Jesus knew God intimately, personally, and, in his case, uniquely as his Father. Can the Christian know God in a similar manner? Years ago, I read in J. I. Packer's book *Knowing God* the following:

> You sum up the whole of New Testament religion if you describe it as the knowledge of God as one's holy Father. If you want to judge how well a person understands Christianity, find out how much he makes of the thought of being God's child, and having God as his Father. If this is not the thought that prompts and controls his

worship and prayers and his whole outlook on life, it means that he does not understand Christianity very well at all. For everything that Christ taught . . . is summed up in the knowledge of the Fatherhood of God. "Father" is the Christian name for God.[3]

I cannot say that I understood those words fully then. But over the years I have come to see with increasing clarity the truth and wisdom of the point Packer is making here. Careful study of the New Testament confirms this beyond doubt. We are not just speaking about God being the Father as the First Person of the Trinity. Rather we are referring to the fact of Christians being given the privilege of calling God our heavenly Father in an intimate and personal manner.

Throughout the New Testament, this truth is clearly taught in a variety of ways. For example, Paul in 2 Corinthians 6:18, rephrasing Isaiah 43:6 in a fresh way for New Testament believers, speaks of God telling his people, "I will be a father to you, and you shall be sons and daughters to me." Or again, the writer of Hebrews, in his challenge to the readers to stand firm in the face of persecution, speaks of the suffering we have to endure as God's way of disciplining his own: "God is treating you as sons. For what son is there whom his father does not discipline?" (Heb 12:7).

Apart from the various incidental references, the New Testament emphasizes this truth in four distinct ways. The first two ways are the images of being "born again" and of "adoption" used by John and Paul respectively. The third is the manner in which Jesus teaches his disciples to address God as Abba, Father, in the same way that he himself did. The fourth is found in Jesus's call to his followers to live their lives completely under God's security and provision. It was through his personal example and teaching that his disciples grasped the truth about their filial relationship with God and learned to appropriate it for themselves. We will now look at each of these in turn.

Born Again

Most of us are familiar with the image of being "born again" in the New Testament. We read this in Jesus's reply to Nicodemus who had come to him by night, "Truly, truly, I say to you, unless one is born again, he cannot see the kingdom of God" (John 3:3). The phrase "born again" can also be translated "from above" (Greek, *anōthen*). In other words, no one can become a Christian

---

3. Packer, *Knowing God*, 182.

and let God reign as King in one's life without experiencing the new birth from above through the Holy Spirit (3:5–8). Peter also used the born-again image, although with a different Greek word (1 Peter 1:3, 23).

This is essentially the same as what John writes in the prologue of his Gospel – "But to all who did receive him, who believed in his name, he gave the right to become children of God, who were born, not of blood nor of the will of the flesh nor of the will of man, but of God" (John 1:12–13). Thus right at the beginning of John's Gospel, this grand truth is stated simply and clearly. All who are in Christ have been born anew into God's family through the power of the Holy Spirit by the will of God.

Adoption

Paul uses the idea of "adoption" (Greek, *huiothesia*) to teach us about our filial relationship with God (Rom 8:15, 23; 9:4; Gal 4:5; Eph 1:5). He explains it as follows:

> For all who are led by the Spirit of God are sons of God. For you did not receive the spirit of slavery to fall back into fear, but you have received the Spirit of adoption as sons, by whom we cry, "Abba! Father!" The Spirit himself bears witness with our spirit that we are children of God, and if children, then heirs – heirs of God and fellow heirs with Christ. (Rom 8:14–17)

However, Paul's image of adoption used here needs some unpacking.

First, adoption in Paul's writings must not be understood in the same way it is practiced today. Adoption nowadays in many cultures involves bringing a baby or child from outside the family into one's own, making them a full member of the family. Paul's image is, however, based on Greco-Roman practices of his time, which differ from adoption practices today in two important ways.

The first difference is that in Greco-Roman practice, adoption involved an adult rather than a baby or child. A man with title and wealth but with no heir would adopt a grown-up person whom he deemed worthy to carry the family name. Adoption bestowed the full privileges of sonship, as well as all the responsibilities of a son and heir. Adoption could also happen if the adopting father had children of his own but deemed none of them worthy to carry the family name. He would then look for some other young man who met his expectation and adopt him as his son. The other difference from modern practice is that once a person was adopted, they could not be disowned and disinherited. In present-day practices, sometimes the adoption goes wrong and the adopted child is marginalized compared to the biological children and treated as less than a full member of the family. Under Greco-Roman law this was strictly forbidden. Whatever happens, the one adopted would retain the full rights and privileges of a son.

Second, in John 3:5–8 Jesus links being "born again" with the work of the Holy Spirit in the believer. It is exactly the same with Paul's idea of adoption. All who know the leading of the Spirit in their lives are the children of God (Rom 8:14). It is through this "Spirit of adoption" that we can cry "Abba! Father" (v.15) and it is this same Spirit who bears witness with or to our spirits that "we are children of God" (v.16).

Third, Paul explicitly reminds us that we have not received a "spirit of slavery to fall back into fear" (Rom 8:15), be it the fear of God's wrath, judgment, sin, Satan, death, or anything else in all of creation (vv.37–39). Rather what we have received is the "Spirit of adoption as sons" (v.15) which makes us "heirs of God and fellow heirs with Christ" (v.17). In other words, when we come to know Christ as Savior we are set free from the fear of and enslavement to sin, Satan, and death, precisely because we have now been brought into God's family as his sons and daughters.

In his novel *Ben-Hur*,[4] Lew Wallace gives a powerful illustration of Paul's theological imagery. Unjustly sent to the galleys as a slave, Ben-Hur is freed by Arrius, a Roman consul and naval commander whom he had rescued in a sea battle against pirates and who then adopted him as his son. As the adopted son of Arrius, he returns to Jerusalem to face his childhood friend, and now enemy, the Roman tribune Messala, who had unjustly sent him to the galleys in the first place. Those who have seen the 1959 blockbuster may remember the scene when Ben-Hur faces Messala, without the fear of a slave and with all the dignity of the adopted son of Arrius, to demand an accounting from him of the fate of his mother and sister. What a powerful image of the Christian life! As Christians we too have been set free from slavery and fear, and can now stand with our heads held high in our dignity as God's children, in defiance of the destructive powers of sin, Satan, and death.

One final point needs noting. In the minds of some readers, the image of our adoption as "sons of God" immediately raises the question of whether the New Testament is gender biased. The answer is pretty straightforward. Adoption as practiced under Greco-Roman law applied only to men and not

---

4. Lew Wallace, *Ben-Hur: A Tale of the Christ* (New York: Harper & Brothers, 1880). Ben-Hur has been made into several films, the most well-known of which is the 1959 blockbuster.

to women. Paul could not have spoken of the adoption of women as "daughters of God" without reducing his language to incoherence in the cultural context of his time. But for Paul, adoption as "sons of God" applies to all Christians, both men and women, who all share fully all the privileges of being a child of God. In fact he makes himself absolutely clear in Galatians where he writes, "in Christ Jesus you are all sons of God, through faith . . . There is neither Jew nor Greek, there is neither slave nor free, there is no male or female, for you are all one in Christ" (3:26, 28). Thus in reading the phrase "sons of God" in the New Testament, the dynamic equivalent in today's language would be "sons and daughters of God," as Paul indicates in 2 Corinthians 6:18.

Abba, Father

The third way in which the New Testament teaches us that God is our Father in a personal sense, and probably the most significant, is Jesus's use of the term Abba.[5] He used this term to address his Father and also taught his disciples to do the same. In the New Testament two words are used for Father: Abba in Aramaic, the lingua franca of Palestine in Jesus's time, and *pater* in Greek. Abba is found three times in the New Testament (Mark 14:36; Rom 8:15; Gal 4:6); and *pater* is commonly used in the New Testament, more than 150 times in the Gospels alone, both for Jesus's relationship with God and also the Christian's relationship with God. In Aramaic, Abba was a term used by both children as well as adult sons and daughters, with a meaning probably best expressed as "dear Father" in English, or "papa" or its equivalent in other cultures. It is not a formal address, but intimate without being over familiar. And this is important in that Jesus taught his disciples to have a personal family relationship with God as our Father.

But there is more. It is now generally agreed that it is the Aramaic *abba* which underlies many of the references to *pater* in the Greek translation of Jesus's words. The importance of Jesus's use has been highlighted by the German scholar of an earlier generation, Joachim Jeremias.[6] He argues that nowhere in the literature of the Jewish people, both inside and outside the Bible, in the thousand years before Christ can be found a single example of the use of *Abba* as one's personal address to God. The reason was that "to the Jewish mind, it would have been irreverent and therefore unthinkable to call

---

5. David E. Aune, "*Abba*," in *International Standard Bible Encyclopedia, Volume One: A–D*, edited by Geoffrey W. Bromiley (Grand Rapids, MI: Eerdmans, 1979), 3–4.

6. Joachim Jeremias, *The Central Message of the New Testament* (London: SCM, 1965), 9–30.

God by this familiar word."[7] He goes on to comment that "It is something new, something unique and unheard of, that Jesus dared to take this step and speak with God as a child speaks with his father, simply, intimately, and securely. There is no doubt then that the *Abba* which Jesus uses to address God reveals the very basis of his communion with God."[8]

There is no doubt that Jeremias's thesis is essentially right, although it needs to be somewhat modified. There is evidence in the Talmud, with roots in the first century BC, that the Jews, especially the Pharisees, sometimes addressed God as Father in the time of Jesus. Nevertheless Jesus's usage was distinctive because he appeared to have changed the occasional invoking of God as Abba in prayer into his typical form of address to God.

But the crucial point here is that Jesus taught his disciples to address God in precisely the same manner as he himself did. The most notable example of this is the use of "Our Father" in the model prayer for the disciples (Matt 6:9; Luke 11:2), which all Christians today recite as the Lord's Prayer. This also brings home to us one more important aspect of this truth that runs counter to what is sometimes believed. Scholars like A. M. Hunter have noted that "Jesus did not speak of God as *Abba*, Father, before all the people . . . The Fatherhood of God was not, therefore, a truth which Jesus proclaimed to all and sundry but a secret he disclosed in private to his disciples."[9] In other words, to call God "Abba, Father," is the unique privilege of those who know Christ personally, and is not for all. In him we have become God's adopted children.

Jesus's Teachings on Our Father's Protection and Provision

Jesus did not just teach us to address God as Abba, Father in an intimate family manner. He goes further to instruct and challenge us to live habitually under the security and provision of the Father, and thereby claim our Christian birthright. This emphasis runs right through his training of his disciples.

Prayer: "Your Father knows what you need"
In teaching his disciples to pray, Jesus tells them not to pray as the Gentiles or unbelievers do, most probably alluding to Elijah's encounter at Mount Carmel with the prophets of Baal and Asherah (1 Kgs 18:26–29). There is no need "to heap up empty phrases" or to use "many words" (Matt 6:7). Why? Because

---

7. Jeremias, *Central Message*, 21.

8. Jeremias, 21.

9. A. M. Hunter, *The Work and Words of Jesus*, rev. ed. (London, SCM: 1973), 76.

"your Father knows what you need before you ask him" (Matt 6:8). Prayer is not an exercise in flattering an egomaniac deity with empty praises until he is fully sated, or groveling after a grudging despot till he finally relents. Rather it is more like a child confidently approaching and talking to "papa" or "daddy" who already knows very well what we need and delights to bestow upon us his generous bounty.

Our daily needs: "Do not be anxious"

Against the background of our human anxieties over the necessities of life including money (Matt 6:19–24), food and clothing (6:25), and health (6:27), Jesus points his disciples to God's adequacy in all these. The birds of the air "neither sow nor reap nor gather into barns, yet your heavenly Father feeds them" (6:26). That the flowers of the field are clothed with greater beauty than Solomon in his finest demonstrates God's all-sufficiency. Therefore the disciples should stop worrying about their daily needs, because "your heavenly Father knows that you need them all. But seek first the kingdom of God and his righteousness, and all these things will be added to you" (6:32–33). In other words, we are called to live with reckless abandon, in radical obedience and trust instead.

Heirs of the kingdom and its authority

In the parallel passage to Matthew 6:19–33 discussed above, Luke includes the following: "Fear not, little flock, for it is the Father's good pleasure to give you the kingdom" (Luke 12:32). Jesus calls his disciples "little flock," and the gift of the kingdom refers to all the blessings of being under God's kingly rule, including the Father's all-sufficient provisions we just looked at. On these all are agreed. What is however missing in modern discussions on this verse is the omission of any reference to the kingdom's authority or power, and to that extent our understanding of Jesus's words is impoverished.

The inclusion of divine authority in Jesus's reference to the kingdom is in fact required by the context because Luke 12:32 is preceded by at least three sets of verses in which the kingdom and authority for ministry and mission are inseparably linked. In Luke 9:1–6 we read that Jesus called the twelve and "gave them power and authority over all demons and to cure diseases, and he sent them out to proclaim the kingdom of God and to heal." When he sent out the seventy-two in Luke 10:1–12, again the link between the power for mission, and healing in particular, and the kingdom is explicit (v.9). Furthermore, in the next chapter Jesus makes the same linkage in his controversy with some unbelieving Jews over his authority to do exorcism: "But if it is by the finger of God that I cast out demons, then the kingdom of God has come upon you" (11:20). A. M. Hunter sums this point up neatly in his explanation of the meaning of the kingdom of God:

> The kingdom of God . . . is the *eschaton* – God's final purpose – invading history. It is God breaking dynamically into human affairs, God's conflict with the powers of evil, through Jesus and his ministry, for men's deliverance, and the new order of things thus established. It is a divine crisis – nay, *the* divine crisis, the crisis which gives meaning to all history before and after it. And, for Jesus, the new order has been decisively initiated in his ministry.[10]

Given the above, it is impossible to deny that the gift of the kingdom to Jesus's "little flock" includes the privilege and right to exercise the Father's authority. Thus, in Luke 12:32, Jesus assures his disciples that the Father has given them the full blessings of living under his kingly rule. Included among these is the Father's authority that empowers them to advance the cause of the kingdom and assures them of victory over all the malevolent forces of sin, Satan, and death.

Our ultimate destiny: "Fear not . . . you are of more value than many sparrows"
The same emphasis on the Father's sovereign care is presupposed in Jesus's instructions to his disciples on how to face persecution in the context of faithful witness (Matt 10:16–33). They do not have to be anxious about how to answer their opponents, however vicious and hateful they may be, because "it is not you who speak, but the Spirit of your Father speaking through you" (v.20). Moreover, there is no need to fear even in the face of death. If not even one sparrow "will fall to the ground apart from your Father," why then should the disciples worry when they are of "more value than many sparrows" (vv.29, 31).

Summing-up

We can now draw the threads together. The language of being "born again" and "adoption," together with Jesus's example and teaching on Abba, show that Christians have been called and brought into an intimate family relationship with God as Father. This points to our fundamental identity. But Jesus does not stop there. Repeatedly in the Gospels, we find him instructing his disciples on how to live as God's children, secure in his Fatherly protection and provisions.

---

10. Hunter, *Work and Words*, 98.

No wonder J. I. Packer, as quoted earlier, could say, "'Father' is the Christian name for God."

Jesus in life, ministry, and mission lived in the full consciousness of his filial relationship with his Father and in the unfailing security of the Father's love. This allowed him to go about life in a calm and cool manner, and gave him inner strength and fearlessness in the face of immense challenges and unrelenting opposition. As God's children we too have been given the wonderful privilege and awesome responsibility of living in exactly the same manner, with Jesus as our model. Each time we pray the Lord's Prayer, with its opening words, "Our Father in heaven," we are reminded of our twin privilege and responsibility. How then shall we live?

Donald Joy, former professor at Asbury Seminary, wrote a book titled *Unfinished Business*[11] to help men deal with their dysfunctional selves and insecurities arising from the wounds of their past. In it he tells of the then-President of Asbury, David McKenna, preaching during the 1983 Ministers' Conference on campus and sharing openly with the hundreds of pastors gathered there about his own wounds and the deep pain of growing up in a broken home. McKenna was speaking on the theme of "Jesus' Credentials for Ministry: Affirmed by God" to draw attention to the importance of our bond with our fathers for the healthy development of our personhood. He noted in particular God's affirmation of Jesus at his baptism, "This is my beloved Son, with whom I am well pleased" (Matt 3:17), and then drew out the full implications that affirmation had for the human Jesus just as his public ministry was about to begin.

> I claim you. I love you. I am proud of you. Everyone needs to belong, to be loved, to be praised. When God says "I claim You," Jesus finds the strength of His identity. When God says, "I love You," He finds the strength of His security. When God says, "I'm proud of You!" He has His sense of worth. This is the unshakable identity that Jesus took as His credentials into His public ministry. We too need these strengths of personhood. These are the relational credentials we must have if our ministry is to be effective: a sense of identity, of security, and a sense of self-worth.[12]

---

11. Donald Joy, *Unfinished Business: How a Man Can Make Peace with His Past* (Wheaton, IL: Victor Books, 1989).

12. Cited in Joy, *Unfinished Business*, 36–37.

Let me hasten to add that what McKenna says here applies equally to women too. What he notes here is essentially on the same page as John 13:3, yet enriching its message from another perspective. Jesus's clarity and confidence in his sense of identity, security, and self-worth gave him the strength to live as a servant in submission to the Father even to the Cross. It is this same sense of identity, security and self-worth that will also sustain us on our journey to the end!

Additional Note: Does Speaking of God as Father Reflect Gender Bias in Our Thinking About Him?

Some readers may have difficulties with the emphasis given here to the Christian's filial relationship with God as Father. In certain cultures this is seen as inappropriate because it gives rise to the impression that God has a male gender. This is a huge topic in itself and there is no way we can go into the details. But nonetheless, some brief comments are warranted.

First, the biblical use of the term "Father" for God employs an image borrowed from human life. It draws on elements such as strength and protection, love and provision from the image of a human father in order to provide insights into the nature of God. But there are also dissimilarities between God our Father and a human father. Nowhere does the Bible encourage us to think of God as male. Indeed there are clear examples of feminine images used to reveal the character of God. For example, the book of Isaiah speaks of God going through the travail of childbirth for Israel's sake (Isa 42:14), whose relationship with her is like that of a mother who has carried her in the womb (46:3), and whose love for Israel far exceeds that of a mother for the child she has suckled (49:15). We find the same emphasis in Jesus's use of the image of a protective mother hen gathering her chicks in his lament over Jerusalem (Luke 13:34). Biblical religion does not encourage us to think of God as either masculine or feminine.

In his *Systematic Theology* the German theologian Wolfhart Pannenberg makes the same point, especially against the polytheistic background of ancient Canaanite religion.

> The aspect of fatherly care in particular is taken over in what the Old Testament has to say about God's fatherly care for Israel. The sexual definition of the father's role plays no part. A mark of Israel's faith from the very outset is that . . . God . . . has no female

partners. To bring sexual differentiation into the understanding of God would mean polytheism; it was thus ruled out for the God of Israel . . . The fact that God's love for Israel can also be expressed in terms of a mother's love shows clearly enough how little there is any sense of sexual distinction in the understanding of God as Father.[13]

Second, we must remember that we have been invited to address God as Father through a gracious act of self-revelation by God. The initiative is entirely God's. And if God has revealed that his nature can best be understood through the image of the Father, then those who take propositional revelation seriously will have to recognize that this is not something that we have a right to pick and choose. Rather, our task is to seek to understand what it is that God intends us to understand through the use of the term Father.

What then is it that God wants us to understand about his own nature when he reveals himself as Father? It appears that what is intended by the term "father" as used here sums up the highest and the best in the combined parenthood of both father and mother in the human family. Thus when we call God "Father," we are addressing neither a male nor a female God. Rather what we are acknowledging is that God is like the very best of human parents in his loving purpose and the exercise of his sovereign power to provide for and to protect us as his children. And it is such a God who calls us into a Father–child relationship with himself, so that we can worship and glorify him on the one hand and fully enjoy him and his mercies on the other.

---

13. Wolfhart Pannenberg, *Systematic Theology*, vol. 1 (Grand Rapids, MI: Eerdmans, 1991), 260.

6

Living in the Security of Our Father's Love

In the last chapter we saw that our Lord Jesus in his incarnate life on earth was fully aware that he was the one of whom the Father declared, "This is my beloved Son, with whom I am well pleased" (Matt 3:17). Confirmed in the consciousness of his filial relationship to the Father, he lived his human life on earth in the security of his Father's infinite power and love. We, on the other hand, although imperfect humans flawed by sin, nevertheless in Christ have been given the unique privilege of having been born again or adopted into God's family. And, as our Lord taught us, we too have been given the special privilege of living in the security of our Father's power and love.

Is it possible then that we can indeed live under the security of our Father in the way modelled for us by Jesus? The answer has to be "Yes" if we are to take the witness of the New Testament seriously, especially our Lord's teachings on the subject. Yet as every Christian who has attempted to live in this manner will tell us, it is far easier said than done. To do so, we need first to know in the depth of our beings what it means to be a child of God and to grow in our relationship with him in life. But unlike Jesus, all of us are dysfunctional individuals, grossly flawed by sin, marred by personal brokenness and deep insecurities. One clear example of this is that children who have been abused – physically, emotionally, sexually, or otherwise – often have great difficulty trusting others both in their childhood and in adult life. Our wounds and insecurities become major obstacles to our growth in trusting our Father in the way that Jesus modelled for us.

In my younger days I was too naïve to understand the problems of human brokenness and insecurities in the depth of our beings. I had done well academically and had a successful youth ministry in my early working life. When the time came to go for theological studies in my late twenties, I went off to Trinity College, Bristol, where some of the leading Anglican evangelical luminaries of the day were then teaching, including J. I. Packer and Colin Brown. I had waited impatiently for five years since graduation to go for pastoral training, but had been held back by personal and family reasons. At last I was free to go with all necessary provisions in place. It was going to be an exciting and enriching time – or, so I thought. Then I fell into a depression within the first year!

Providentially, the lecturer for pastoral counselling was the late Dr. Monty Barker, a consultant psychiatrist and an adjunct faculty member of the medical school in Bristol. I had gotten to know him personally and, after lunch one Sunday afternoon, he sized up my problem within an hour. He helped me understand the traumas of my growing up in a high-achieving but dysfunctional family. He further helped me see that all my human accomplishments would at best serve as a cover-up for the deep unresolved insecurities, but could never help me overcome them. That was the beginning of a long pilgrimage over many years during which God slowly worked in me the healing of my inner brokenness and insecurities.

Just as importantly the whole experience opened my eyes to the fact that, even if we are unaware of them, all of us harbor wounds and insecurities in our lives, some more and others less. Sometimes through fortunate circumstances in life such as growing up within a loving home and with adequate finances, or through personal achievements in public life and the like, it is possible to cover up some of these but never everything. And inevitably everyone is crippled to a lesser or larger extent, unless healing is found in Christ. If we are to live in the security of God's love as Jesus did, the first thing we have to do is to face the truth about ourselves.

Facing the Truth about Our Brokenness and Insecurities

Many years ago, a professor of pastoral counselling from a leading evangelical seminary in Canada was speaking to the students in the seminary where I was then teaching. He told our students that many in pastoral ministry were themselves deeply wounded and insecure people. Without knowing healing in their lives it would simply not be possible for them to be effective ministers of the gospel and bring healing to others. When pressed he said something that was even more troubling. Based on his observations in his own seminary in Canada, he estimates that some 80 percent of all trainees go through their training without addressing their personal issues and leave with their broken lives unhealed. If this is true of pastors and church workers who have the opportunities to be exposed to these matters through their studies in counselling and spiritual formation, what about the average church members who don't?

In our study of the description of Jesus in John 13:3 in the last chapter we noted how Jesus, secure in his Father's love, was untroubled by the basic insecurities that drive human lives. He knew who had ultimate control over his life, he had a clear sense of his identity as God's beloved Son, and he was absolutely sure that he could trust his Father with his final destiny. On the other hand, as flawed humans our lives are often driven by our insecurities and fears over these same basic issues. These insecurities manifest themselves in many and different ways. A brief look at some examples of how these insecurities work themselves out in human lives will help us better understand our human predicament.

Human Insecurities

In the previous chapter we compared the response of the twelve disciples at the Last Supper with that of the over a thousand boys in my old school. We saw in both cases how peer pressure and the need to preserve our self-image in the eyes of others played a crucial role behind our fears and the inability to do what is right. This of course gets played out in countless ways in everyday life. No one likes to be an oddball, no one enjoys going against the tide. It is much easier to be politically correct and more convenient to just follow the crowd. The same insecurity, rooted in our deep-seated need for acceptance, often lies behind the incessant chase after positions, titles, status symbols, scholastic attainments, promotions, and bigger pay packets. For many in leadership, this also drives our quest for popularity on the one hand and inability to take correction and constructive criticism on the other.

Closely related are the questions regarding our identity and origins that plague us consciously or sub-consciously far more than we dare admit. I write this at a time when the emotions over the callous death of an African American, George Floyd, exploded as Black Lives Matter demonstrations spread across America and the rest of the world. But fears of rejection and victimization are not just about race and skin color. They are also about family lines and marital connections, the schools we attended and universities we graduated from, the firms we work for and the like.

Insecurity about money is another major driving force in many lives. Some grow up poor and have experienced the painful rejection and shame of poverty.

Their consequent insecurity about not having enough leads them to place the pursuit of wealth at the top of their life agenda. Others grow up rich but have been taught since they were young that the social standing they enjoy is all about money. So they too are driven by the same insecurity in order to get the respect they crave. And many of us are plagued by the fear that failing to live at the same standards as our neighbors is a mark of social and cultural inferiority. Such insecurities lie behind the covetousness and mindless pursuit of wealth by many.

Still others are insecure about power, hence the power-crazy syndrome in many leaders' lives. They grab every position they can and hold on to them tightly, even if their usefulness in them has long expired. Some strive to be perceived as superstars or all-powerful CEOs so that they can maintain control over their mini-empires and have the last word in every decision. Such people will always have difficulty functioning in a team without being in control. The results can be devastating. The sight of insecure pastors and lay leaders, for example, leaving behind a trail of messed up churches, not to mention deeply hurt individuals, is unfortunately too common in today's world. I know of one such person splitting three churches in succession.

Then there are those who are insecure in relationships. Marriage counsellors can tell endless stories about spousal relationships thoroughly messed up by the insecurity of one or both partners. Mission history is littered with stories of insecure parents stopping their children from leaving home for ministry overseas because they are desperately hanging on to them. Similarly, in many parts of the Majority World where the pastoral vocation does not command high social standing or great pay packets, many Christian parents oppose their children going into ministry out of fear that their children will not have enough to provide for them in their old age. They may love Christ deeply themselves, but their insecurities over relationships and money lead them to go against God's will for their children's lives.

Finally, insecurities over the future haunt us all. Will or will I not make it to the top of the pile in my profession and work so that I will look good before my peers and in the world? Or, especially in difficult times, such as the coronavirus pandemic we are in at present, with a major recession hanging over the world economy, the concern can be the more mundane one of whether we will have enough for our families today and for ourselves to retire on tomorrow? And of course there are always the inescapable questions posed by our frail mortality, disease, old age, and death.

The above is only a tiny sample of the concerns that drive our deep-seated insecurities in life. Nevertheless, all these revolve around the three fundamental insecurities of life, namely, who has ultimate control over my life, what is my fundamental identity, and what is my destiny both in this life and beyond? John 13:3 informs us that Jesus was able to transcend these because he lived constantly in the security of his Father's love. Can we live in the same manner too? Before we answer this question we need to note one more thing.

Our Insecurities and Our Inner Wounds

The pervasiveness of sin, and its devastating effects on human life, is such that all of us, without exception, are spiritually and emotionally damaged people. The consequence is that our insecurities are further aggravated by the inner wounds and brokenness of our lives.

We have noted, for example, that Jesus operated out of a clear sense of identity and affirmation by his Father. Many of us on the other hand are always desperately struggling with self-acceptance because, owing to uncertainties and confusion about our self-identity, we are constantly plagued by self-rejection. Such feelings of self-rejection are often traceable back to our formative "growing-up" years. Stephen Seamands, in his book *Ministry in the Image of God*, states:

> The seeds of self-rejection from which the false self emerges are generally planted in our formative childhood years. As a result of our dysfunctional family life, a lack of unconditional love and experiences of personal trauma, a false self takes root and develops to alleviate our pain and meet our needs for love, intimacy, affirmation and acceptance.[1]

Hurts and wounds in later years and our wrongful responses to them, such as unforgiveness, unresolved anger, and bitterness, exacerbate the problem further.

If we learn to live in the security of our Father's love, we must be prepared to face the reality about our dysfunctional selves. This is the first step and, to be honest, it is a big one. The uncomfortable truth is that many of us are so damaged and insecure that we have unconsciously built a thick wall around our inner self in order to protect ourselves from being hurt further. In our mind the fault is always with someone else, for to admit to any shortcomings and brokenness on our part would mean that we would need to begin dismantling

---

1. Stephen Seamands, *Ministry in the Image of God: The Trinitarian Shape of Christian Service* (Downers Grove, IL: InterVarsity Press, 2005), 130.

this thick wall that we have mentally and emotionally built to protect the frail and deeply wounded individual within.

Many are too fearful to take that step because doing so would mean exposing their broken selves and making themselves vulnerable. Some are also held back by pride that prevents them from admitting their own weaknesses and the ugly sides of their lives. The late psychiatrist and pastor, John White, in his book *Changing on the Inside*, draws our attention to another still more basic reason why we find it painful to face the reality about our dysfunctional selves, namely the fear that we will not be loved.

> In the depth of our being . . . all of us have an insatiable craving to be loved. And we have a deep-down fear that we won't be . . . Without love we begin, quite literally, to die. For this reason, all of us harbor a terrible fear of rejection. We may be unaware of this craving for love and fear of rejection. They may be buried deep in our unconscious minds. Yet subtly and powerfully, these feelings influence our behavior and distort our view of life around us . . . This deep and insatiable need for love and the consequent fear of rejection lie at the root of our difficulty in facing reality, as well as our difficulty in changing. There are things about ourselves and the people in our lives that we dare not face, because at a deep level we are desperately afraid that reality involves not getting the love we need.[2]

In line with Seamands's comment on self-rejection quoted earlier, White too points out that the severity of our problem goes back to our early childhood. "The earliest events in our lives are crucial. Being loved inadequately likely produces damage throughout our development, certainly well into our adolescent years. And the earliest damage is the most dangerous."[3]

Yet unless we are willing to face the truth about our broken lives, we will never know healing and change. Many have seen case after case of pastors, for example, messing up their ministries and prematurely giving up, or being forced to give up their calling because they find it too difficult to confront their inner wounds and pains. Unless the individual is willing to expose themself, the love of Christ and the healing power of the Spirit cannot access the wounded

---

2. John White, *Changing on the Inside: The Keys to Spiritual Recovery and Lasting Change* (Guildford, Surrey: Eagle, 1991), 41.

3. White, *Changing on the Inside*, 41.

person within. Many go through their lives without experiencing the power of the Christ to heal and transform.

The consequence is that in the lives of many Christians, including many in leadership, the effectiveness and impact of their ministries are badly crippled by their wounds and insecurities. Because they are compromised, their ministries reach a certain level beyond which they cannot go, however gifted they may be. Like an eagle with damaged wings, even if it can still fly, it can never soar!

Dealing with the wounds and hurts of our dysfunctional selves is a huge subject and clearly lies outside the scope of this book. For the reader who is seeking help in this area of life, speaking to a wise pastor, counsellor, spiritual director, or even just a mature friend who is seasoned enough to understand your problem is a good place to start. Reading carefully some good books on the Christian ministry of healing and praying through the issues as the Holy Spirit brings them to your attention will greatly help.[4] Having a network of close friends or a small group who can minister to you through prayer, provide emotional support through more difficult moments, and hold you accountable to deal with wrongful responses such as unforgiveness and resentment will go a long way to ensuring that you are moving in the right direction.

But if we are serious in wanting healing, we must be prepared for the long haul. Because so much of our brokenness is deeply embedded in our memories of the past, healing takes time. But as John White, puts it, "Only the experience of a loving Christ can heal such a memory. And this is why I insist on the church's role in such healings. It is also why I declare that healing is a sanctifying process."[5] Thus an essential part of the process of growing wholesome and holy and more like the perfect human Jesus is to know healing for our dysfunctional selves. When that begins to happen, we will also find ourselves more and more able to live in the security of our Father's love.

------

4. On the healing of the wounds and hurts on the inner person, see, for example, Leanne Payne, *The Healing Presence* (Eastbourne: Kingsway, 1989), and *Restoring the Christian Soul: Overcoming Barriers to Completion in Christ through Healing Prayer* (Grand Rapids, MI: Baker, 1996); David A. Seamands, *Healing for Damaged Emotions*, 3rd ed. (Colorado Springs, CO: David Cook, 2015); Steve Seamands, *Wounds That Heal: Bringing Our Hurts to the Cross* (Downers Grove, IL: InterVarsity Press, 2003); John White, *Changing on the Inside: The Keys to Spiritual Recovery and Lasting Change* (Ann Arbor, MI: Servant Publications, 1991), and *Eros Redeemed: Breaking the Stranglehold of Sexual Sin* (Downers Grove, IL: InterVarsity Press, 1993).

5. White, *Eros Redeemed*, 193.

Living under Our Father's Security

Having learned to face the truth about ourselves, the next step is to get to know God as Father. At the risk of oversimplifying, allow me to suggest some simple steps. These steps are not necessarily consecutive. As with so many things in life, they are likely to overlap each other.

Knowing Who We Are

The first step in the journey of learning to live under our Father's love is to know who we are in Christ. We could just as well have titled this section as "Know Your Rights and Privileges." Do we consciously live as a child of Abba, Father? Allow me to repeat some things already noted earlier. John reminds us that "to all who did receive him, who believed in his name, he gave the right to become children of God" (1:12). This verse, together with what has been said about the terms adoption and Abba, reminds us that in Christ we have the right, power, or authority (Greek, *exousia*) of a child to go to God our Father.

The whole emphasis is on our right and privilege of access to God, as children having the right of access to our fathers. Hence Paul speaks of Christians not having "the spirit of slavery to fall back into fear, but . . . the Spirit of adoption as sons by whom we cry, 'Abba! Father!'" (Rom 8:15). Without intending any flippant sense of over familiarity, the point is, do we know what it means to address God, not just Abba, Father, but also "papa" or "daddy," or their equivalent in our heart language? The early church fathers in recognition of this truth prefaced the Lord's Prayer with the words, "We make bold to say, 'Our Father'!"

Philip Yancey in his book *What's So Amazing about Grace?* recounts a story about the Oval Office when John F. Kennedy was president of the United States. With all the protocol and tight security, no one could expect to get into the president's office easily or unannounced. But there appear to have been exceptions. Every now and then, in the midst of all the weighty matters of the state being deliberated by the cabinet, John-John, the two-year old toddler son of the president, would be seen crawling all over the huge presidential desk, oblivious to everything else going on! The toddler knew daddy and was just visiting as usual.[6]

Knowing who Abba, Father, is and having boldness in our access to him makes all the difference in prayer. In the story of the healing of Lazarus who

---

6. Philip Yancey, *What's So Amazing about Grace?* (Grand Rapids, MI: Zondervan, 1997), 157.

had been dead for four days, Jesus approaches the tomb and prays, "Father, I thank you that you have heard me. I knew that you always hear me." And with that he commands, "Lazarus, come out" (John 11:41–43)! How often have many of us wished that we too can pray with such confidence and authority? That is the model Jesus sets for us. Why settle for less?

Down the ages there have been those who have learned to pray with such a sense of unimpeded access to our Father, just as little toddler Kennedy knew unimpeded access to his father in the presidential office. Some who have understood prayer in such a manner may be like Billy Bray, the converted coalminer and Methodist lay preacher from Cornwall, England, who was known to say whenever an issue came to him, "I must talk to Father about that." Others who have gone further along in the life of prayer may be as audacious as Moses who, having been assured that God's presence would go with him and the Israelites in their journey to the promised land, pressed ever closer to God and asked for the ultimate gift, "Show me your glory, I pray" (Exod 33:18 NRSV)! Those who know such boldness of access to the Father will indeed see something more of the glory of God.

Entering Deep into Our Father's Love

Learning how to pray boldly is one thing; making a conscious effort to enter more deeply into the Father's love as his children is another. Where do we begin? Many have made the point that we need to know God's unconditional love. I must confess that I sometimes cringe when I hear this from some writers and preachers, especially those whose theological framework is shaped more by modern pop psychology than the Bible.

To speak of God's love as unconditional without qualification is misleading. It negates the central message of the Old Testament prophets. This was the call to Israel to return to her covenant commitments as the condition for enjoyment of the blessings of God's covenant with her. It also negates the message of Christ, whose opening line in his ministry is, "The time is fulfilled, the kingdom of God is at hand; repent and believe in the gospel" (Mark 1:15). Yes, the Bible tells us that "God showed his love for us in that while we were still sinners, Christ died for us" (Rom 5:8). God's offer of salvation to us is entirely at his own initiative and made without any prior conditions. But there is no running away from the simple fact that unless there is repentance and a returning to God on our part, we can never know the salvation offered in Christ and enjoy the love of God that comes with it.

Once we are clear about the fundamental need for repentance, there is a real sense in which God's love is unconditional. It is that we are accepted as we are, and not because of who or what we are by virtue of some qualities, things, or achievements we have. We are accepted through faith in Christ and nothing else.

Many struggle with this, especially those who have never known their parents' unconditional love. To press home the point, Jesus tells a story commonly called the parable of the prodigal son (Luke 15:11–32). That is probably a misleading title because the central character in the story is not the rascal but the father. Many commentators and preachers fail to capture the full force of the story because they focus on the guilt of the son rather the pain and shame suffered by the father. The story would be more appropriately titled the parable of the waiting father, as suggested by Helmut Thielicke, the German theologian and preacher, in his book on Jesus's parables.[7]

Set in an ancient Palestinian community, or for that matter in any traditional small town or village in many parts of the Majority World today, the action of the son would have been a major scandal. All the neighbors would be whispering and gossiping among themselves about this disgraceful family with a useless father who cannot even bring up his son properly. In societies where a strong shame culture prevails, the only way to protect the family's honor is for the son to be publicly disowned. Nevertheless, the father, who is broken-hearted yet without bitterness and rancor, bears and absorbs the shame fully in his own being as he waits patiently for the son's return. Finally one day the rascal appears in filthy rags, truly repentant though still smelling of the pigsty. Yet the father rushes forward to hug and kiss him, and throws a party for the whole town to celebrate the homecoming of his lost son. That is what the unconditional love of our waiting Father is like! He bears the pain inflicted by our sin through the cross, absorbs the shame, waits patiently for our return, and sets no limits on the blessings he purposes to impart.

If we would enter deeper into the love of the Father, we need to come to God in this manner and no other, even if we are in spiritual rags and still smelling of the pigsty. We would also need to learn the discipline of waiting upon God in quietness, consciously resting in his love, and yearning to know more of his presence. This means setting aside time to seek him daily and regularly taking days off for spiritual retreats. And be ready to welcome his

---

7. Helmut Thielicke, *The Waiting Father: Sermons on the Parables of Jesus* (London: James Clarke, 1960).

loving presence at any moment because he never fails to surprise us, often when we least expect him!

When we do these things we will begin to understand what Paul means when he speaks of God's love "being poured into our hearts through the Holy Spirit who has been given to us" (Rom 5:5). It would be the beginning of a deep-seated healing process for the wounds and brokenness of our lives without which we cannot be made whole. It would set us on the path of living freely under the security of our Father's love and in turn empower us to impart God's love and healing to others.

Our Father's Absolute Determination to Watch over Us

Side by side with entering deeper into God's love, we also need to grow in our confidence in God's absolute determination to care for us and provide for our needs. In the context of teaching his disciples about the place of prayer in their lives, Jesus comments, "If you then, who are evil, know how to give good gifts to your children, how much more will your Father who is in heaven give good things to those who ask him" (Matt 7:11). The point is that sinful as we are, as parents we always seek to give our best to our children. How much more then will our holy Father give of his best to each of us?

There is a truism accepted by community development workers worldwide: One of the most important means of bringing development to the poor is to educate women. Why? Because educated mothers (never mind the fathers, regretfully) will not only make sure that their children get educated, but they will also be better equipped to give their children what is best for their nurture.

Many years ago when our firstborn was barely eighteen months old, my wife and I took him to the local wet market. My wife was in one part of the busy market and our son was with me in another section. I had taken my eyes off him for a few moments to rearrange the shopping basket and then when I turned around he was gone! I panicked as I had not done for years because there were numerous cases of missing children at that time. For the next few minutes I searched frantically for him in the crowd and then to my great relief, I saw him with my wife. She had bumped into him happily wandering among the fishmongers, spellbound by the variety of fishes he had never seen before, happily oblivious of his father's anxiety.

As we drove home that morning, I remarked to my wife that we must never let him out of our sight again. No sooner had I finished saying that – there was no lightning in the sky, no thunder in the air – I heard God's unmistakable word to me: "If you love your son so much, how much more do you think I love you?" It was unforgettable!

Martin Luther is by common consent the theologian par excellence of the sixteenth-century Reformation. Unfortunately, most of the time we forget that he was also a spiritual giant who knew and trusted his God deeply. How else could he have had the courage to lead the battle for both the revival and reform of the church in his day when the forces aligned against him included both the emperor and the pope? We earlier referred to his stunning conduct at Worms in 1521. But three years before that he had been summoned by papal order for a hearing before a Cardinal Cajetan at Augsburg. He was a marked man and many of his friends and supporters pleaded with him not to go, fearing that he would never return. But Luther would have none of that.

On his way to Augsburg, his German advisers warned him that all his enemies wanted to do was to burn him at the stake. His reply to them gives us the true measure of the man and his faith: "If my cause is lost, the shame is God's."[8] The Reformation scholar, James Atkinson, in his book *The Great Light: Luther and Reformation*, comments, "This indeed is a text for Luther's life. It is not his cause but God's and God is faithful to those He calls."[9] But there is more. As the Reformation battle raged on, Luther continued to give both theological leadership and pastoral guidance to the reforming party through his books and letters. Atkinson goes on to comment that what is striking in all these writings is "Luther's inextinguishable faith and invincible confidence. He wrote and talked as a man whose cause would never fail . . . There is about Luther that disconcerting certainty . . . He said he was a detached observer watching a cause that could only prosper."[10]

Clearly Luther knew in his life something of his Father's utter determination to watch over him and ensure the success of the cause that God had entrusted to him.

Is Abba Father BIG Enough?

To live under the security of our Father involves grasping clearly our identity as a child of God, entering deeper each day into his love, and knowing his utter

---

8. Cited in James Atkinson, *The Great Light: Luther and Reformation* (Exeter: Paternoster, 1968), 50.

9. Atkinson, *Great Light*, 50.

10. Atkinson, 103–4.

determination to watch over us. How do these work out in real life? Can we just trust the Bible's bare words?

Many of us who are parents will no doubt remember teaching our young children how to ride a bicycle. Their first question is, "Won't I fall down?" Telling them about Newton's laws of motion and the mathematics involved is clearly a non-starter. The only answer we can give is, "Try it!" In the same way when we ask, "How can we be sure that Abba Father is big enough to deliver?" His answer thunders back, "Try me!"

This has been the same story down the ages. When Gideon was called out of obscurity to deliver Israel from the hand of the Midianites, four times he had to ask for assurance that God was big enough (Judg 6:17, 36–40; 7:9–14), including the repeated miracles of the dry and wet fleece. When God rebuked Israel through the prophet Malachi for their failure to honor him with their tithes and offerings, he also challenged his people to try him. "Bring the full tithe into the storehouse, that there may be food in my house. And thereby put me to the test, says the LORD of hosts, if I will not open the windows of heaven for you and pour down for you a blessing until there is no more need" (Mal 3:10).

Earlier in the previous chapter we examined how Jesus in particular taught his disciples about their filial relationship with God their Father. He did not just teach them to address God as Abba, Father. He taught them how they should live out this spiritual reality of being God's children by trusting him in their day-to-day living. Thus prayer becomes for us a family conversation in which we can go with confidence to Abba, Father because he knows what we need even before we ask (Matt 6:8). And since our Father knows what we need, we can therefore live in radical obedience and complete trust, and not be weighed down with constant anxiety (6:25–34). Moreover as heirs of the kingdom and entrusted with divine authority (Luke 12:32) we need not fear all the malevolent forces ranged against us in life. Come what may, our eternal destiny is safe in our Father's hands (Matt 10:16–33). Or, as George Whitefield puts it, "We are immortal until our work on earth is done."

The principle of trusting a God who is big enough to provide is well illustrated in modern times by the faith missions. Take the China Inland Mission (CIM), the first truly interdenominational mission society in the world, now known as OMF International.[11] It was founded by Hudson Taylor (1832–1905) on the principle of never publicizing its needs but looking to God

---

11. The name was first changed to Overseas Missionary Fellowship, and it is now called OMF International.

alone through prayer to provide. It was the Protestant mission that impacted China most, being the first to penetrate every province with the gospel even before Taylor's death in 1905.

There is a delightful story about Taylor that illustrates the principle of living under the security of the Father's love beautifully. He arrived in China in 1854, barely twenty-two years old. Having done five years of medical training, he was still six months short of completing his medical diploma. But he had decided to leave early for China in response to a sense of urgency in his missionary call. There he met Maria Dyer, an orphan of missionary parents, who was under the guardianship of the very formidable Miss M. A. Aldersey. The latter was very much against Maria marrying Taylor, and did everything possible to oppose the match. In her mind, among other things, he was an unconnected nobody, without title, whether "Rev." or "Dr.," and without the support of an established missionary society. But as the saying goes, "Man proposes, God disposes." Once Maria's uncle in London gave his approval, the wedding was all set.

As the day drew close, there was only one problem. They had no money, not even enough to pay the marriage license fee! Then a gift came out of the blue and the immediate issue was resolved. But Hudson Taylor, recognizing the difficult journey ahead of living without assured financial support, wanted to give Maria one last chance to back off from her commitment if she felt that that was too much for her. He said, "You see how difficult our life may be at times." Her simple reply will remain one of the classic statements of Western mission history and a fitting summary for this chapter: "I have been left an orphan and God has been my Father all these years. Do you think I shall be afraid of trusting him now?"[12]

Concluding Thought

A colleague of mine recounted a story from an American pastor with whom he had stayed while studying in the USA. One day this pastor was home alone with his little daughter. He had left the little girl on the ground floor while he went down into the basement. The ladder-like stairs leading to the basement had been damaged, and to repair them, he had to remove them. Then it happened – there was a power failure and the whole house went dark. With the stairs dismantled, he could not immediately get back to the ground floor. Meanwhile his daughter was looking for him in the semi-darkness, calling

---

12. Cited in A. J. Broomhall, *Hudson Taylor and China's Open Century: Book Three, If I Had a Thousand Lives* (London: Hodder & Stoughton, 1982), 121.

"Daddy! Daddy! Where are you?" So he called out to her saying, "I am here. Just follow my voice." At last the little girl appeared and stood hesitantly at the edge of the basement trapdoor. The father could see her tiny figure clearly silhouetted against the dim light from outside and knew that he could safely catch her if she just jumped. On her part, all the little girl looking down could see was a big black hole. Then she heard daddy's gentle voice, "Darling, I can see you. Just jump!"

Jesus in his incarnate life knew his Father's voice when he heard the words, "This is my beloved Son, with who I am well pleased." Like Jesus and also the little girl, we too need to know our Father's voice. The Christian life is not, as some cynics suggest, a leap in the dark. Rather, because we have learned to recognize our Father's voice, it is a leap into his strong and loving arms!

"My sheep hear my voice, and I know them, and they follow me." (John 10:27)

7

But the Lord Looks on the Heart

Time magazine did a "Quick Take" piece on 28 September 2015 titled, "Good Leaders Don't Have to Be 'Good,'"[1] by Jeffrey Pfeffer, a professor at Stanford's Business School. Pfeffer notes that many exponents of leadership studies, including Jim Collins, stress the fundamental importance of virtue and traits such as "authenticity, modesty and concern for others." But he argues that this is simply not true to life because many industrial and political leaders have few, if any, of such qualities. Instead, he states, "The vast majority of research shows that narcissism, rather than modesty, predicts being selected for and surviving in leadership roles . . . Sometimes, the best bosses have to lie and manipulate to save money and jobs. Often, they have to disregard concern for others." He also refers to a *New York Times* piece on Machiavelli that concluded that history shows that virtue often leads to ruin, "whereas pursuing what appears to be vice results in security and well-being."[2]

Pfeffer's views may well be shared by many in corporate circles, politics, and elsewhere. Many think that what has been said in earlier chapters about servanthood and submission is totally impractical in life. In the rat race for supremacy, many nations and corporations focus on building up their talent pool to provide themselves with the most talented leaders to advance their agendas. They look for the smartest and toughest, but not necessarily the most virtuous. After all, the virtuous are often not the best equipped to increase shareholder value in corporations or win elections in politics.

Unlike Pfeffer, however, I am addressing this book primarily to Christians who seek to serve Christ in the church or Christian organizations. At the end of the day you will have to decide for yourself whether what is written here

---

1. Jeffrey Pfeffer, "Good Leaders Don't Have to Be 'Good,'" *Time*, 28 September 2015, 15.
2. Pfeffer, "Good Leaders," 15.

also applies to Christians in business and politics. In response to Pfeffer I have three things to say.

First, if our call is to servanthood and that entails submission to our Father, then clearly Pfeffer's worldly-wise views have to be ignored. I am not denying what he asserts about his views being backed by the "vast majority of research" and that they actually work in the world. I am simply saying that for the Christian who takes the call to discipleship and servanthood seriously, character and holy living have to be central to one's thinking and motivation. A narcissistic servant of Christ in pursuit of vice is simply an oxymoron.

Second, what Pfeffer says does not relate in any way to what we have referred to as spiritual authority in chapter 3. For the Christian who seeks to tap into the powers of heaven and exercise genuine spiritual authority, enough has already been said to indicate that one cannot simply side-step the issues of virtue and character. How else can there be a genuine submission to the will of the Father that alone makes that possible?

Third, like Pfeffer, the Bible is interested in the leadership question although, as we have seen, the perspective it takes is quite different from that of the world. In various places, biblical writers are concerned with the question of what kind of person best qualifies for leadership in the work of God. For example, in the Old Testament Moses is described as "very meek, more than all the people who were on the face of the earth" (Num 12:3). And when Samuel came looking for the next king in Jesse's house, he was told explicitly by God that "man looks on the outward appearance, but the LORD looks on the heart" (1 Sam 16:7).

As for the New Testament, we have already seen what Jesus expected of his disciples and those who aspire to service in the kingdom. But we need also to note what Paul says about what qualifies a person to govern or have oversight in the church of God. In his instructions to both Timothy (1 Tim 3:1–13) and Titus (Titus 1:5–9) on the appointment of overseers (elders) and deacons, there is general agreement among commentators that the primary qualities sought in the candidates are spiritual and moral, and not talent, education, and social standing.

What is clear from the above is that again and again, for those charged with leadership in the work of God, the Bible's emphasis is on the central importance of character and spiritual qualities. Nowhere is this clearer than in Paul's farewell speech to the Ephesian church elders in Acts 20:17–35, which we shall now look at in some detail.

But before doing so, we need to come back once more to Pfeffer. He asserts that in the real world character and virtue often have to be replaced by deceit and manipulation. Right? Interestingly, *Time* magazine in the immediate next edition came out with the story of Volkswagen's (VW) Dieselgate scandal of 2015 that made headlines all over the world.[3] Was this coincidental or providential? The lawsuits against VW are still ongoing globally at the time of writing this, with final penalties likely to cost the car maker tens of billions of dollars.

If the VW scandal is an isolated case, little more need be said. But in the past two decades we have had a number of high-profile accounting scandals involving huge multinationals, as well as the subprime mortgage crisis of 2008 caused by the proliferation of unregulated financial derivatives that nearly crashed the world banking system. At the root of all these is the fact that integrity and virtue had been tossed out by corporate leaders in pursuit of profit margins and shareholder value. Pfeffer's view raises the fundamental question of whether the world economic order of the twenty-first century can survive without having at its heart integrity and virtue, which alone can ensure that trust, justice, and fair play will prevail. I will have to leave it to others far more qualified than me to answer this. But if the corporate collapse of entities like WorldCom and Arthur Anderson, the 2008 subprime banking crisis, and VW's Dieselgate are things to go by, then the answer seems pretty obvious.

Character and Servanthood in Paul's Life

Luke's account of the apostle Paul's farewell address to the leaders of the Ephesian church is one of the classic statements about what servanthood means in the ministry of the church. Paul visited Ephesus on his third missionary journey and helped establish the church there (Acts 19). Now on his way back to Jerusalem he meets up with the Ephesian church elders (20:17) or overseers (20:28) for one more time. Sensing the difficulties ahead, which might mean that they will never meet again, he speaks to them in words summed up in Acts 20:18–35.

It is likely that Luke's summary of Paul's parting address here is representative of what Paul said to all other churches to which he was bidding farewell. Here he shares openly from his heart about what he has sought to accomplish in his work among them as an evangelist and a pastor, the inward and outward struggles that he faced constantly, and the cost to himself of faithfulness in ministry. And as their spiritual father, he further charges them

---

3. Matt Vella, "A Diesel Deception at VW Shows New Curves Ahead for Carmakers," *Time,* 5 October 2015, 7–8.

to remember his personal example and to be alert in watching over their flock. We will examine Paul's address, not by way of a verse-by-verse exposition, but by highlighting five marks of what being a servant in Christ meant for him and, by implication, for us.

"Serving the Lord with All Humility"

Paul begins by noting that his life has been transparent before the Ephesian church and that they have seen him "serving the Lord with all humility" (Acts 20:19). Significantly, the first thing that Paul speaks of is humility, the opposite of pride. Knowing something about his background tells us that the battle against pride in his life would not have been won easily. What else can we expect from someone who comes from the untainted cultural line of "a Hebrew of Hebrews," a Pharisee who can boast of his fanatical religious zeal as "a persecutor of the church" and of his "righteousness under the law, blameless" (Phil 3:5–6), and whose academic credentials are such that even his Roman judge, Festus, shouts at him publicly saying, "Paul . . . your great learning is turning you mad" (Acts 26:24 RSV)?

In the Bible, pride has always been seen as, in today's parlance, the "mother of all sins"! As one scholar sums it up, "In relationship to God pride is lofty self-sufficiency; in relationship to other persons pride is haughty lack of concern for their well-being . . . Thus the proud person offends against God by self-exaltation, against other people by self-preoccupation, and against the self by self-deception."[4] None of us are free from it, and few, if any at all, are conscious of how strongly entrenched it is in the depth of our being. As C. S. Lewis puts it, "There is no fault which makes a man more unpopular, and no fault we are more unconscious of in ourselves . . . If you think you are not conceited, it means you are very conceited indeed."[5]

None of us in spiritual leadership are exempt from this besetting sin. If we are honest, we see this at every level of ministry and leadership in the church and Christian organizations. And the higher we go up the hierarchy, the worse the temptations and the manifestations get. The only way to combat this is to consciously strive for humility. Three things, at least, are needed in its pursuit.

---

4. Judith E. Sanderson, "Pride; Proud," in *International Standard Bible Encyclopedia, Volume Three: K-P*, edited by Geoffrey W. Bromiley (Grand Rapids, MI: Eerdmans, 1986), 960.

5. C. S. Lewis, *Mere Christianity* (London: Collins, 1952), 106, 112.

Doing the lowly but needful tasks

The first is to be willing to do that which is lowly but needful. Most of us, by nature, love attention and the limelight that give us a sense of affirmation and self-importance. This is of course further aggravated by the increasingly competitive cultural environment in which many of us grew up. Our natural tendency is to avoid lowly, even if needful, tasks and anything that does not help raise our public profile.

Take for example what Paul says to the Ephesian elders about teaching "in public and from house to house" (Acts 20:20). If we are honest, most of us crave to teach and preach in public. But how many would want to do so "from house to house"? In my part of the world, I get told by church members in middle-class churches that some pastors do not believe in house visitations anymore. I don't think this is a problem only in my part of the world. Evidently pastors and church leaders have other more important things to do nowadays. But evidently that is also one reason why the level of Christian discipleship is declining all over the world.

One of the most effective means of battling pride is to seek out and perform tasks that may appear lowly but are needful. A man I know is an archbishop in a very important diocese of the Anglican Church worldwide. We were working together on the committee of a global evangelical movement, and at one meeting a long and messy set of minutes of over twenty pages had to be cleaned up. Without much ado, he simply volunteered, "I will fix it." By the next morning it was done. I asked someone from his church about him and her comment was, "He is always like that with a servant's heart."

Some would know the story that René Padilla, the late Latin American missiologist, tells of how he and John Stott once arrived at a conference site late at night and had to walk through pouring rain and mud to get to their room. Next morning when he got up, he saw Stott cleaning his shoes. Over his protestation, Stott simply responded, "My dear René, Jesus told us to wash one another's feet. Today we do not wash feet the way people did in Jesus's day, but I can clean your shoes."[6]

Appreciating the contributions of others

In Jim Collins's study *Good to Great*, he notes that Level 5 leaders are not just humble and modest, but that one of their characteristics is that of constantly

---

6. René Padilla, "Jesus Told Us to Wash One Another's Feet . . . I Can Clean Your Shoes," in *John Stott: A Portrait by His Friends*, edited by Chris Wright (Nottingham: Inter-Varsity Press, 2011), 121.

"looking out of the window" rather than "looking at the mirror." What he means is that these leaders will look beyond themselves through the "window" to attribute credit to others or to external circumstances when things go well, but will look at the "mirror" to take the blame when things go wrong. Comparison leaders will do exactly the opposite of taking credit for themselves when things go well and shifting blame to others or circumstances when things foul up.

How often do our senior church leaders and pastors of big churches look out of the window, rather than into the mirror, to credit others for their contributions? In Paul's letter to the Philippians, he urges them to "Do nothing from selfishness or conceit, but in humility count others better than yourselves" (Phil 2:3 RSV). It took me years to fully grasp Paul's meaning here. Within the body of Christ, everyone has been blessed with some gifts for the work of ministry (1 Cor 12). While some gifts may be more spectacular or more public than others, each person's area of gifting is just as significant and important. And often what appears to be of lesser significance may well produce greater impact in the work of the kingdom.

Among those I remembered most during my university days are a couple who opened their home every Saturday evening to international students for their Christian fellowship meeting over a period of thirty years. On a rough estimate, probably a couple of hundred students found Christ through those home meetings and many hundreds more received encouragement and inspiration to grow deeper in faith. Perhaps I have stronger public ministry gifts. But who am I to dare think that their gift of hospitality ranks lower in God's eyes? In fact, the impact of their hospitality gift remains for me a powerful model even today for outreach to international students the world over.

In the eighteenth-century evangelical revival in Britain, the two outstanding evangelists were George Whitefield and John Wesley. Although they remained friends, there was always a simmering tension between them caused by Wesley's semi-Arminianism as against Whitefield's Calvinism. And, unfortunately, their respective followers were prone to stoke the flames every so often. Some in Whitefield's camp went so far as to suggest that Wesley might not be truly converted, and one even asked Whitefield whether he expected to see Wesley in heaven. Whitefield's reply is instructive: "I feared not, for he will be so near the eternal throne and we at such a distance we shall hardly get a sight of him!"[7]

Stories like this are, regretfully, far from common. Church leadership is so often marked by hubris and a lack of genuine respect for colleagues and those

---

7. Cited in Arnold Dallimore, *George Whitefield: The Life and Times of the Great Evangelist of the Eighteenth Century Revival*, vol. 2 (Edinburgh: Banner of Truth, 1980), 353.

supposedly under our care. Does this not indicate a failure to fully appreciate the contributions of others, however insignificant they may be in public eyes? How much greater unity there would be in the work of the kingdom if we are able to demonstrate a similar respect and generosity towards those whom we would, in our weaker moments, consider competitors in ministry?

Self-effacement

A third mark of humility is self-effacement, the ability to remain modest and avoid attention-seeking. This is indeed a challenge in today's environment. From the time we start school, if not before, we get drummed into us the message that if we wish to get anywhere in life we must demonstrate our worth, advertise our achievements, and blow our own trumpets, even if discreetly. In a world characterized by padded résumés to enhance career advancement, a "publish or perish" mindset in academia, and pastors and preachers incessantly proclaiming their own exploits, whether it is about their congregation numbers or the signs and wonders they claim to have performed, self-effacement makes little sense. Yet, against this cacophony we hear Paul saying, "But I do not account my life of any value nor as precious to myself, if only I may finish my course and the ministry that I received from the Lord Jesus, to testify to the gospel of the grace of God" (Acts 20:24). His life and public ratings are really secondary so long as the job gets done!

It is however to Barnabas in the New Testament that all of us owe the most challenging lesson in self-effacement. Barnabas was the one who introduced Paul, the former persecutor of Christ's followers, to the Jerusalem church leaders at a time when no Christian there would have anything to do with him (Acts 9:27). It was Barnabas who brought Paul in to help strengthen the rapidly growing church at Antioch (11:25–30). When the time came for the Antioch church to send out Barnabas and Paul (13:2, 7) as missionaries, it was Barnabas who was in the lead with his name coming first. But following the encounter with Elymas the magician on Cyprus (13:6–12), the name order changed to Paul and Barnabas (13:50). Eventually after the Council of Jerusalem (Acts 15), there was only Paul and no Barnabas.

Here we see a powerful example of self-effacement. It is not about who is in charge or has the prominence. It is rather who is best suited for a particular task in the kingdom which matters. Without Barnabas there would never have been a Paul. Yet when the time came, Barnabas knew how to get out of the way so that the Holy Spirit could have full freedom to work through Paul – who was once a junior colleague. No wonder the apostles nicknamed him "son of encouragement" (Acts 4:36).

I know a missionary couple called to Colombia in 1976 at a time when the drug cartels ruled the land. As with other missionaries, their work aroused opposition. The husband was targeted and nearly killed but for the car door which stopped the bullet meant for him. God told them to pray for revival and to raise up younger people for ministry in the church. When revival finally hit Colombia after some twenty years, they left for another difficult mission field because God told them that their work in Colombia was done. Many in their situation would have stayed to enjoy the adulation and earthly fruits of their labor. Could it be that one test of true humility is whether we are willing to work ourselves out of our jobs?

Luke's description of Paul is a call to us to seek to serve the Lord "with all humility." What is suggested here is that the battle against pride has to be consciously fought and that true humility is found only if it is actively sought. Charles Simeon, the great Cambridge preacher of nineteenth-century England, had an amazing ministry there of fifty-four years, so much so that when he died the whole city shut down for his funeral. In one of his letters to an older friend he observes that many young pastors are fond of talking about "that great letter 'I.'" He then goes on to say, "the three lessons which a minister has to learn: 1. Humility. 2. Humility. 3. Humility. How long are we in learning the true nature of Christianity!"[8]

Pastoral Compassion

The second important mark of a servant is compassion. Paul speaks of serving God not just in humility but also "with tears" (Acts 20:19), and that he "did not cease night or day to admonish every one with tears" (20:31). These remarks reveal not just his humanity but also his compassion for those under him. The concern for pastoral compassion is also seen in his charge to the Ephesian elders to watch over the church with the caring heart of a shepherd: "Pay careful attention to yourselves and to all the flock, in which the Holy Spirit has made you overseers, to care for the church of God, which he obtained with his own blood" (20:28).

Most of us who seek to do well in ministry, especially those aspiring to leadership roles, are passionate people. After all one can hardly do anything well without passion, although we will need to learn to bring our passions into line with God's purposes. However, what is often missing in our lives is compassion, and with it the capacity to empathize with the weak, slow, and

---

8. Cited in Handley C. G. Moule, *Charles Simeon* (Leicester: Inter-Varsity Press, 1948), 65.

stubborn. I know from personal failure how easy it is to be firm and hard, to scold, criticize and rebuke. But how often have we wept for those who are broken beyond self-help, or living with unnecessary self-inflicted pain, or unrepentant and self-destructing as a result?

A friend who once visited Israel relates the following incident. The tour guide on the coach was telling the group that in Israel shepherds never herd sheep by driving them from behind with a stick or whip. Rather, he gently leads the sheep from the front. Just then the coach passed a man driving a bunch of sheep in front of him and that of course made the tour guide rather embarrassed. So he stopped the coach and went over to talk to the man driving the sheep. Moments later he came back with a broad smile on his face and told everyone: "It is alright. That is not the shepherd. He is the local butcher!" That says it all, doesn't it? How do our colleagues and those under our care think of us? Shepherd or butcher?

Faithfulness in Ministry

Discussions and books on ministry tend to focus more often than not on the issue of success, measured by evangelistic breakthroughs, number of converts and church plants, projects accomplished, and the like. Measured by these, there is no doubt that Paul was successful. Yet in his farewell address to the Ephesian elders there is no mention of these things at all. Instead he shares with them about how tough things have been at times in the past as he speaks of the "trials that happened to me through the plots of the Jews" (Acts 20:19). He does not expect things to be any easier going forward given that "the Holy Spirit testifies to me in every city that imprisonment and afflictions await me" (20:23). That being the case, he therefore urges them to watch over the Ephesian church because of the dangers he foresees coming both from within and without (20:28–30). Paul spoke about three things in particular.

Faithfulness in face of opposition

The first concerns faithfulness even when the going gets tough. The constant focus on success in many of today's churches would probably have distressed Paul because of the opposition to the gospel he and the other apostles had to contend with daily. He himself had previously been guilty of persecuting the church and played an active role in Stephen's martyrdom (Acts 7:58). He certainly would also have known of James's martyrdom (12:2). Moreover, in his own life as a Christian he had to endure similar persecutions, as well as the difficulties and the personal cost incurred through his missionary work. These are all spelt out clearly in four passages in the Corinthian correspondences (1 Cor 4:9–13; 2 Cor 4:7–12; 6:3–10 and 11:21–29), with the last probably clearest. In it he speaks of the fact that, compared with those falsely claiming to be apostles, he has had to pay the price of true apostleship with

> far more imprisonments, with countless beatings, and often near death. Five times I received at the hands of the Jews the forty lashes less one. Three times I was beaten with rods. Once I was stoned. Three times I was shipwrecked; a night and a day I was adrift at sea; on frequent journeys, in danger from rivers, danger from robbers, danger from my own people, danger from Gentiles, danger in the city, danger in the wilderness, danger at sea, danger from false brothers; in toil and hardship, through many a sleepless night, in hunger and thirst, often without food, in cold and exposure. (2 Cor 11:23–27)

Yet in the face of all this, he did not flinch but faithfully persevered in order that "I may finish my course and the ministry that I received from the Lord Jesus, to testify to the gospel of the grace of God" (Acts 20:24).

Adoniram Judson (1788–1850) was one of the founders of the Student Volunteer Movement that sent out tens of thousands of missionaries from North America in the nineteenth century. In a missionary career spanning thirty-eight years, he pioneered the beginnings of the Burmese church though he only saw a handful of converts. Charged with being a British spy during the First Anglo-Burmese War he was incarcerated for twenty-one months, hung upside down every night in leg irons. He lost two wives in succession and six children, plus numerous coworkers, but nevertheless managed to complete a Burmese dictionary (1824) and the translation of the first Burmese Bible (1840). Probably not a great success story in some church circles today. A few years ago, one visitor to Myanmar (formerly called Burma) asked a local pastor about Judson. With tears in his eyes he replied, "Today there are six million Christians in Myanmar, and every one of us traces our spiritual heritage to one man – the Reverend Adoniram Judson."[9] Somewhat overstated perhaps, but the point is well made.

You probably will not read most of the examples given in this chapter in the books touting the leadership and success agendas today. But without persevering in faithfulness amidst opposition down the centuries, how far

---

9. As told by Paul Borthwick; cited in Lindsay Brown, *Shining Like Stars: The Power of the Gospel in the World's Universities* (Nottingham: Inter-Varsity Press, 2006), 172.

would Christian mission have gone? The Chinese church is probably one of the fastest growing and most vibrant in the world today in spite of the continuing state-driven persecution. One aspect of their missionary vision is the "Back to Jerusalem" movement by which some are seeking to bring the gospel back to all the countries along the old silk routes, both on land and by sea. This will mean going through the heartlands of Buddhism, Hinduism, and Islam, which remain to this day some of the toughest mission fields in the world. This vision was first pioneered way back in the 1920s by the indigenous Jesus Family church, whose motto was "Sacrifice, abandonment, poverty, suffering, death."

Preaching "the whole counsel of God"

Faithfulness for Paul also means not holding back from "declaring to you anything that was profitable" (Acts 20:20) or hesitating to preach "the whole counsel of God" (20:27). Every faithful pastor or preacher understands what Paul is talking about here, together with all the pressures and apprehensions involved. Preaching and speaking God's truth to any congregation requires not just prophetic courage but also pastoral sensitivity. There are times where one has to tread carefully between the two, and the ever-present temptation and danger is always wanting just to be a nice guy. Sadly, this appears to be why many have allowed their weekly sermons to stoop to the level of ego massage or Sunday entertainment to draw the crowds. Such preachers remind us of J. B. Phillips's paraphrase of Hosea's indictment of the unfaithful priests of his days: "They have changed a glorious calling into a shameful trade" (Hos 4:7).

Those called to servanthood in the kingdom will have to courageously face up to this challenge from day-to-day. Was it easy for Nathan, the prophet, to confront David, the king, over his twin guilt of adultery and murder? In my own context, I have often found it difficult to preach on certain subjects like corruption to Christian business circles in Asia or power abuse to church leaders. But there are times when pastoral responsibility demands the exercise of prophetic courage even when you feel timid as a mouse! And you cannot shrink back even if after the sermon you get told, as some of us no doubt have been, that "If that is how you preach you won't be invited back."

Sacrifice

In the above discussion on faithfulness we have already noted something of Paul's sacrificial way of life. We come now to the part of his address where he informs the Ephesian elders that he is heading towards Jerusalem, not knowing what is in store there. He prepares himself for the worst. Nevertheless, under the compulsion of the Spirit he must go (Acts 20:22–25). But what makes it possible for Paul to function in this manner is the conviction that "I do not account my life of any value nor as precious to myself, if only I may finish my course and the ministry that I received from the Lord Jesus, to testify to the gospel of the grace of God" (v.24). It was this single-mindedness and absolute obedience to Christ that made Paul who he was.

How many in today's church understand such a spirit of obedience and sacrifice? Yet if we examine carefully the stories of those who have had real kingdom impact, again and again we will find lives of great sacrifice. We referred in chapter 3 to John Sung whose ministry in the late 1920s and 1930s manifested powerful evangelistic, prophetic, and healing gifts, and brought revival to many Chinese churches throughout China and parts of Southeast Asia. The son of a Methodist pastor, he arrived in the USA with broken English in 1920 and yet sailed through his university studies all the way to a PhD in less than six years. A brilliant academic career lay before him. But he set that aside in response to God's call pressing heavily upon him and returned to China in 1927. In the next fourteen years he literally burnt his life up for the advance of the gospel and helped lay the foundations for the explosion of the Chinese church in the second half of the twentieth century. His active ministry only ended in late 1940 when an unhealed surgical wound from his student days in America finally got so bad that the fistulas eventually grew to a foot (30 cm) deep.[10] He languished in that condition until his death in 1944. But his work was done.

Writing in the foreword of the first English biography on Sung, John Stott quotes James Denney's words, "There must be great renunciations if there are to be great Christian careers."[11] Will the global church in our century have the privilege and joy of seeing a deluge of great Christian careers laboring together for the advance of the gospel? The answer will depend on how much we are willing to pay the cost of spiritual greatness.

---

10. Sung, ed., *Diary of John Sung*, 408. Although the English translation does not have the full details given in the original Chinese text.

11. Cited in John Stott, "Foreword," in *John Sung: Flame for God in the Far East*, rev. ed., edited by Leslie T. Lyall (London: Overseas Missionary Fellowship, 1956), viii; reissued as *A Biography of John Sung* (Singapore: Armour, 2004), xxxiii.

No Place for Self-Seeking Ambition

We come finally to the fifth mark that Paul notes in Acts 20, which is the need to guard against self-seeking. This manifests itself in many forms. For example, in May 2018 it was widely reported that one North American televangelist openly appealed to his supporters to buy him a new $54 million Falcon 7X private jet. His justification for asking, which he states whimsically with a straight face, is that "If Jesus was physically on earth today, he won't be riding a donkey. Think about that."[12] Sadly, those who are familiar with the churches around the globe know that this is not just an American problem!

Paul concludes his address to the Ephesian elders with the words:

> I coveted no one's silver or gold or apparel. You yourselves know that these hands ministered to my necessities and to those who were with me. In all things I have shown you that by working hard in this way we must help the weak and remember the words of the Lord Jesus, how he himself said, "It is more blessed to give than to receive." (Acts 20:33–35)

The contrast between the televangelist and Paul could not have been sharper!

Paul is addressing here the issue of financial covetousness, which is one example of self-seeking ambition. But the same principle applies whether it is money, sex, or power. Billy Graham once said something to the effect that sex is the cause of failure for some three-quarters of American pastors who fall. I am not familiar with other parts of the world, but in Asian churches, probably a majority of leaders fall because of either money or power abuse or both, the latter due in part to the hierarchical authority patterns in our cultures.

Moreover, the problem of self-seeking affects all Christians, whether serving Christ full-time in church or some Christian organization, or on a voluntary basis. Those in church ministry will always be tempted to climb the ecclesiastical ladder to get into positions that give greater power, status, and financial reward. Lay people may not want to be pastors or full-time ministry workers, but many seek positions in churches and Christian organizations because they enjoy the power and prestige that go with them. None are exempt. Like humility, the only way to fight it is to die to self in whatever way the word of God commands or the Spirit's prompting demands.

---

12. *CBS This Morning*, "Televangelist Jesse Duplantis seeks $54M private jet," 30 May 2018, https://www.youtube.com/watch?v=GsQo2TrvYcA; see also "US Preacher Asks Followers to Help Buy Fourth Private Jet," *BBC News*, 30 May 2018, https://www.bbc.com/news/world-us-canada-44305873.

Here again, we can learn something from the apostle's example. In Acts 20, Paul does not only speak against covetousness (v.33), but also tells how he is working hard to help the weak in accordance with the Lord's teaching that "It is more blessed to give than to receive" (v.35). Note that he is not talking about working hard in preaching the gospel, which he certainly did. Rather he is speaking of working hard in his tent-making trade (Acts 18:3) by which he both supported himself in missionary work and also helped the needy.

During the years of his itinerant ministry, John Sung visited many impoverished Chinese churches in China and Southeast Asia. There were times when the local organizers of his revival campaigns would run short of funds. He was known to have actually forked out money from his own pocket to ensure that the campaigns could go on uninterrupted. Evidently, unlike many of today's televangelists and church leaders, Paul and Sung knew what it means to fight self-seeking through self-giving.

There is an exemplary story about E. Stanley Jones (1884–1973), an American missionary of over fifty years in India and a brilliantly innovative and contextual evangelist. On one of his furloughs home in 1928, he attended the General Conference of his own denomination, which was then in the process of electing a new bishop. When the election was deadlocked, someone proposed Jones's name. He was immediately elected by acclamation. But he could not sleep the whole night. The next day, just before the consecration took place, he asked for permission to speak on a matter of high privilege. He thanked the conference for the honor bestowed him and assured them of his deepest respect for the bishop's office. Then he said, "But I am called to be an evangelist and a missionary, and I hereby resign as a bishop-elect of the Methodist Church."[13] Just imagine how much time, energy, and good-will would be saved at election times in our churches if each of us know what our calling in Christ is and stick to it, regardless of the attraction of better prospects or the negative consequences.

Christian Character Formation

When it comes to the choice of leaders for the church or those called to spiritual oversight over God's people, there is a general tendency today to follow the thinking of the world, which prioritizes talent and ability. In contrast, the primary qualifications for leadership and the oversight of God's people in

---

13. E. Stanley Jones, *A Song of Ascents: A Spiritual Autobiography* (Nashville, TN: Abingdon, 1968), 210. This story has been corroborated by other sources.

the Bible are spirituality and character. This emphasis, as I have argued, is clearly seen in Paul's parting speech to the Ephesian church elders wherein he draws our attention to some essential qualities that must characterize a servant of God. These include humility, pastoral compassion, faithfulness in face of opposition, sacrifice, and dying to self-seeking. This is not a comprehensive list but it says enough.

Working largely in the Asian context, I have for a number of years concluded that the greatest need today in Asian churches is for men and women of genuine Christian character. Admittedly, I am less familiar with churches in other parts of the world, although I have lived ten years of my adult life in different parts of the West. But there is enough in the media to tell us that the needs all over are probably no different. For the servant of God, there is no running away from the centrality of character and spirituality in one's life. But character and spiritual maturity do not emerge overnight. Certainly they cannot be attained with a mere three or four years of training, even at the best theological college or seminary. It is a lifelong process through which God works in the depth of our being until Christ is formed in us (Gal 4:19). As one traditional Chinese saying goes, "It takes ten years to grow a tree but a hundred years to cultivate a person."

Those who allow God to do his deep work in their lives will be transformed more and more into the likeness of our Master. They will be confident, yet humble; strong, yet gentle; visionary, yet never riding rough shod over those who disagree; warm, loving, and, in some cases, even commanding personalities, yet never seeking to be idolized; filled with a burning passion for Christ, yet never lacking compassion for the slow and the weak; capable and perhaps highly gifted, but always with the heart of a servant; filled with the Spirit, yet always marked with the meekness of Christ!

How does this transformation process come about? There is actually plenty of material on this in the Bible itself. For those who truly desire to be his servants, God will actively work to break the dysfunctional selves within, and then lovingly reshape and mold us into the persons he wants us to be. Of course we can reject God's work in us and God gives us the freedom to choose. In that case we will never get to where he wants us to be. But for those who are willing to let God have his way in us, we will be totally surprised by what we find at the end of that process. It is to this that we will now turn.

8

The Father's
Transforming Process

The Roman Catholic Church and Eastern Orthodoxy both hold a similar belief in the sinlessness of Mary, the mother of our Lord, although theologically they explain it in slightly different ways. Most Christians outside these churches do not go so far as to assert her sinlessness. But they would almost certainly agree with Geoffrey W. Bromiley that Mary's one outstanding characteristic is "her faith in God" that "evidences itself in her humility, obedience, praise, and familiarity with the OT."[1] We see this in her response to the angel's Annunciation, "Behold, I am the servant of the Lord: let it be to me according to your word" (Luke 1:38), and also in her song of praise, the Magnificat (1:46–55). In any case, the angel's word to her that "you have found favor with God" (1:30), as well as her relative Elizabeth's greeting, "Blessed are you among women" (1:42), clearly point to a special standing before God.

Down the ages, there are probably others who have been blessed in a similar fashion. Unlike most of us who are dysfunctional in varying degrees, now and then we meet some who through the grace of God have grown up in godly and loving homes, and are relatively (though not absolutely) untroubled by the brokenness and insecurity that beset the rest of humanity. Some of these individuals have been further blessed with an intimacy with God early in their life. Mary appears to be counted among such.

In contrast however, most of us under the ravage of sin have often grown up broken, insecure, proud, stubborn, unrepentant, and the like. Before we can be changed into the likeness of Christ, God has to do some deep-rooted work

---

1. Geoffrey W. Bromiley, "Mary the Mother of Jesus," in *International Standard Bible Encyclopedia, Volume Three: K-P*, edited by Geoffrey W. Bromiley (Grand Rapids, MI: Eerdmans, 1986), 269.

in us. The Bible provides many examples of this. In this chapter we will look at how God worked in four different individuals and, as if almost against their will, turned them into people that they may never have imagined themselves to be. We will conclude by looking at a fifth person who willingly embraced God's purpose for his life at a young age and, despite the great pains that his obedience involved, found himself wonderfully transformed to serve God's greater purposes for Israel. Before we explore these stories, we need first to address the prior question of why God would bother to change us at all.

Our Father's Determination to Change Us

So why would God bother with us, especially when all too often we are unwilling partners in the change process? The simple answer is that because we are in his family, our Father is determined that we become mature sons and daughters. His purpose is that we be "conformed to the image of his Son" (Rom 8:29).

The letter to the Hebrews also speaks of this formation process, which God is doing in our lives. Writing to Christians whose faith is being tested under persecution, the author challenges them to faithful endurance and not to lose confidence, even as Jesus endured the cross (Heb 12:1–4). And because they are his children, God is actually using the experience of persecution to discipline and train them for their well-being. Thus he writes:

> And you have forgotten the exhortation that addresses you as children – "My child, do not regard lightly the discipline of the Lord, or lose heart when you are punished by him; for the Lord disciplines those whom he loves, and chastises every child whom he accepts." Endure trials for the sake of discipline. God is treating you as children; for what child is there whom a parent does not discipline? If you do not have that discipline in which all children share, then you are illegitimate and not his children. Moreover, we had human parents to discipline us, and we respected them. Should we not be even more willing to be subject to the Father of spirits and live? For they disciplined us for a short time as seemed best to them, but he disciplines us for our good, in order that we may share his holiness. (Heb 12:5–10 NRSV)

Here the writer uses persecution as an example of the broader principle of how God disciplines us "for our good, in order that we may share his holiness." The word discipline in some contexts today has taken on strong negative overtones. But that is not the intention of the writer. The Greek noun *paideia* (12:5, 11), carries the meaning "the act of providing guidance for responsible living, upbringing, training, instruction"; and the corresponding verb *paideuo* (12:6, 7, 10), means "to assist in the development of a person's ability to make appropriate choices, practice discipline."[2] Although at times the idea of correction through punishment is there, the overall purpose is positive, which is to effect life maturity and character formation. Moreover, as the quote from Proverbs clearly indicates, the disciplining process is done by a loving Father to a "son in whom he delights" (Prov 3:12).

So God seeks to transform us because he is determined to bring about the emergence of mature men and women in his family who are holy and conformed to the image of Christ. He is actively at work to bring this about in each person who has chosen to follow him. However, the problem that our Father confronts is that as soon as he starts this formation process, we start squealing and squirming away, and often do our level best to reject his discipline at every point – because it is invariably painful and uncomfortable. But without his intervention our sanctification will get nowhere.

Four Lives: The Father's Breaking and Transforming Process

To see more clearly how God goes about the change process in human lives, we will look at the lives of Jacob, Moses, Peter, and Paul in turn. We will examine how God goes about cracking the dysfunctional selves, exposing the mess under each false persona, before he reorders and rebuilds them into something holy and wholesome.

Jacob – the Deceiver and Cheat

We begin with Jacob, Abraham's grandson and the third of Israel's patriarchs. He was born, the second of twins. His name, Jacob, means "he takes by the heel" or "he cheats" (Gen 25:26).[3] One day he takes advantage of the careless presumption of his older brother, Esau, in a moment of hunger and exhaustion, and tricks him into selling away his birthright for a bowl of stew (Gen 25:29–34). Then as Rebekah's favored son, he connives with his mother to steal the paternal blessing of his father Isaac for the firstborn from Esau (Gen 27). This paternal blessing not only had legal force in ancient times but also, within

---

2. BDAG, 748–49.

3. Taken from the note on Gen 25:26 in the margin of the ESV.

the patriarchal narratives, designated the heir to the divine promises given to Abraham and Isaac. In short, he stole the two things that really mattered legally and spiritually from Esau.

Jacob is a cheat, a deceiver. In my part of the world, he is called a "snake." But God too has his ways. He simply allows Jacob to be packed off by his mother for his own safety to his maternal uncle, Laban, from a vengeful brother. But there Jacob meets his match. Instead of finding safety he meets a bigger "snake" in his uncle. After paying the bride price with seven years of hard work, he gets tricked by Laban into marrying the wrong woman, and then gets entrapped by his uncle into working another seven years for the younger sister he really wants (Gen 29 and 30).

Six more years of hard work under a difficult and dishonest boss followed before Jacob concluded that enough is enough. He flees with his wives, children, and everything he has without informing his uncle because he fears that he would be stopped (Gen 31:31). But what does the journey home hold? Despite his best efforts to appease his aggrieved brother, he hears that Esau is meeting him with four hundred armed men (32:6). What a welcome! Laban he has left behind, and now he has no choice but to face Esau. God's work of breaking Jacob is slowly but surely being brought to a climax. Caught between the rock and a hard place, the snake has nowhere to turn.

Although in times past Jacob had been aware of God's providential care and gracious provision, yet it is only now that we finally find him desperately seeking God for help (Gen 32:9–12). In his prayer he acknowledges his unworthiness of God's goodness, pleads for God's deliverance against a brother he had wronged greatly, and finally learns to claim God's promises for him and his family. God had to bring Jacob to the end of his own strength and cleverness before he could be changed. In the past Jacob had wriggled his way through life with his cunning and wit, but not now.

Still God is not done with him yet. That same night, left alone at the banks of Jabbok, Jacob finds himself wrestling with a total stranger who dislocates his hip. By then it has finally dawned on him who the stranger is. When asked by the stranger to release his grip on him, Jacob then replies with a combination of audacity and humility, "I will not let you go unless you bless me" (Gen 32:26). But God has one more thing to do. He asks Jacob, "What is your name" (32:27)? Strange question! "Doesn't God know my name?" We often overlook God's sense of humor here. He brings Jacob to the point when he has to confess without any more self-justification who he really is: "Yes, I am Jacob, a deceiver, a snake!" Only then God's work in him is done. Only then is Jacob ready to make a fresh start with a new name: "Your name shall no longer be called Jacob, but Israel, for you have striven with God and with men, and have prevailed" (32:28). Only then could God give Jacob the blessing that he wanted so much and without which it would be disastrous to move forward (32:29).

Moses – the Egyptian Prince

We come next to Moses, several generations after Jacob. Born a son of slave laborers, he is providentially brought up in the palace as an Egyptian prince (Exod 2:1–10; cf. Heb 11:23–25). A thousand years earlier, Cheops or Khufu in the twenty-sixth century BC, had built the Great Pyramid, one of the Seven Wonders of the Ancient World. In Moses's time, Egypt was one of the most advanced civilizations in the world and a regional power. Given the privileges and pleasures of a palace upbringing, Moses exudes learning, confidence, and class. So when he comes to know his own people's suffering and with all that he has by way of natural endowments and palatial training, he seeks to solve their problem by his own strength. He secretly kills an Egyptian taskmaster to protect one of the Hebrews but then has to flee Pharaoh's wrath when that is leaked out.

He runs off to Midian in northwestern Arabia, marries a shepherd girl and settles down there for the next forty years herding goats and sheep. Through those long years, something changed. The desert is a strange place. Moses may have grown up in the palace, brimming with confidence and exuding class, but that almost certainly means nothing in the desert in which he finds himself. You can have all the learning of Egypt under your belt but that is practically useless against the harsh and austere demands of desert life. You may own a Porsche or Ferrari, but neither would be a match for an old weather-beaten camel for going places. In forty years he probably saw little other than sheep, goats, and sand. All these would have led to a shattering loss of confidence in himself and all the pride of Egypt he had imbibed.

The net result is that Moses is no longer so sure of himself as when he killed the Egyptian in his younger days. Thus when God calls him to lead his people out of Egypt, he has excuses aplenty: "they will not believe me or listen to my voice" (Exod 4:1), "I am not eloquent" (4:10), and "please send someone else" (4:13). No doubt a major reason for his reluctance to do what God calls him to do is the loss of confidence in himself. But that also means that he is now a humbler man. We see this clearly in later accounts. When he finally gets down to the task of leading Israel out of Egypt, instead of self-assertively taking his own initiative, we see him regularly waiting on God and meeting him "face-to-face" (33:11) for direction. We also see this new humility in his life in his relationship with others. Not long after the Red Sea crossing, sibling rivalry rears its ugly head. Miriam and Aaron, both Moses's seniors, gang up to challenge his leadership (Num 12:1–16). But he responds by simply leaving his vindication to God, rather than engaging in a family fight. Hence the biblical writer's comment: "Now Moses was very meek, more than all the people on the face of the earth" (12:3).

But there is another positive side to his forty-year exile in the desert that often goes unnoticed. In the later accounts, we read of him speaking to God face-to-face, as well as twice going up Mount Sinai to meet with God for forty days each time (Exod 24:18; 34:28), fasting throughout, at least on the second occasion if not on both. Anyone who is into the quest for a deeper spirituality and prayer life would understand that such practices do not just come overnight, as if beginning only from the time of Moses's call at the burning bush. Without the regular practice of fasting, for example, it is simply not possible to go into a prolonged fast even for a week, let alone forty days. Clearly the narrative shows that he has grown deep in his relationship with God in a way that few others have, one that must have been nurtured through the long desert years.

So Moses has lost confidence. There is no way he can imagine himself doing what God is asking him to do. Mission impossible! But that is exactly where God needs Moses to be. So long as Moses's confidence is in himself and in what Egypt gave him, there is no way that God could use him. His pride and confidence must first be broken. In any case, what can a bunch of runaway slaves do against Egypt's military might? If the exodus is to succeed, it has to be the result, not of any human effort however incredible, but of God's alone! Only thus humbled and transformed is Moses ready to be sent by God with divine authority to say to Pharaoh, "Thus says the LORD, the God of Israel, 'Let my people go!'" (Exod 5:1).

Peter – the Self-Made Man and Born Leader

Like Moses, though in a different manner, Peter too has to go through a humbling process. Of course his education at the local synagogue school of his youth is nothing like Moses's palatial training. When called by Jesus, he was in his twenties or early thirties and running a successful fishing business with his brother Andrew. But he is a self-made man and a born leader. Whenever the disciples are listed, whether in part or in full, Peter's name is always first (e.g. Matt 4:18–22; 10:2). He seems to have acted as the spokesman for the

Twelve (e.g. Mark 8:29, 32; 9:5). Unfortunately, he has a tendency to be too sure of himself as when he tells Jesus at the Last Supper, "Though they all fall away because of you, I will never fall away" (Matt 26:33). So he fails to heed Jesus's warning that that "this very night, before the rooster crows, you will deny me three times" (26:34). When the crunch comes, he goofs – three times. The rooster crows and his eyes meet Jesus's look across the room, and then he remembers. "And he went out and wept bitterly" (Luke 22:62).

The story of Peter's restoration is beautifully told in John 21. There on the shore of the Sea of Galilee, three times Jesus asks him, "Peter, do you love me?" And in response to each of Peter's three unambiguous affirmations, "I love you," Jesus commissions him afresh repeatedly to watch over the emerging church. Though he is grieved that Jesus puts the question to him thrice as a gentle reminder of his failure, nevertheless he knows that he is forgiven. Failure, together with the subsequent restoration and recommissioning, changes him.

Acts tells us that in the early years, Peter is still the leader of the Jerusalem church. But we find him a different man. First, he is no longer so sure of himself and is now more willing to listen to others. Some years later, when the whole Jewish-Gentile question exploded in the church, he allows himself to be corrected publicly by Paul, a fellow apostle (Gal 2:11–14). Perhaps the change is most evident in the gentleness and humility of an older Peter. Once upon a time, he not only always needed to be first, he was also aggressive and impulsive. We see this in his attempt to fight off the soldiers that came to arrest Jesus, cutting off the ear of the high priest's servant in the process (John 18:10). But by the time he writes 1 Peter, he is no longer the same. With a gentle, pastoral heart he exhorts his fellow elders to watch over the flock, to do so willingly and not for personal gain, and to lead by example and not in an overbearing manner (1 Pet 5:1–3). And towards the end of the letter, he urges them to be humble, something that was clearly lacking in himself in his younger days: "'God opposes the proud but gives grace to the humble.' Humble yourselves, therefore, under the mighty hand of God so that at the proper time he may exalt you" (1 Pet 5:5–6).

There is another, even more important, change in Peter. As the New Testament church grew, the leadership of the Jerusalem church and Gentile mission passed respectively into the hands of James, the brother of Jesus, and of Paul. Was Peter sidelined? Unlikely! New Testament scholars like Ralph P. Martin and others have actually suggested on good grounds that Peter may have actually been the indispensable "bridge-person" between Jewish and Gentile Christianity, holding the two factions together despite their massive cultural differences threatening to tear them apart.[4] This would also explain the tradition of his pre-eminent role in the church in Rome where tensions between the Jewish and Gentile Christian communities persisted for some time, as commentators on the book of Romans have noted. If this is correct, it means that, as Peter matured, he came to understand that in serving Christ you can play a crucial and indispensable role in God's purposes without needing to be numero uno, number one.

Paul – the Righteous Pharisee

We come finally to Paul who had a strict Jewish religious upbringing and clearly took great pride in it before his conversion. In his letter to the Philippians, he asserts that if salvation is by human efforts, he stands on firmer grounds than most: "If anyone else thinks he has reason for confidence in the flesh, I have more: circumcised on the eighth day, of the people of Israel, of the tribe of Benjamin, a Hebrew of Hebrews; as to the law, a Pharisee; as to zeal, a persecutor of the church; as to righteousness under the law, blameless" (Phil 3:4–6). Born a member of the chosen race, schooled in its proudest traditions, customs and language (in contrast to Hellenized Jews), and a member of the Pharisaic community (which saw themselves as the holy "separated ones" who observed the law more diligently than all other Jews), he was so religiously zealous that he took the lead in persecuting Christians who were perceived as deviants from Judaism.

Furthermore, he had studied under Gamaliel, the most famous rabbinic teacher of his day (Acts 5:34; 22:3). Whether he was a member of the Sanhedrin, the Jewish ruling council, at a relatively young age has been debated. But he certainly had close connections with it and access to its leading members. This is evidenced by the fact that he guarded the clothes of those who killed Stephen by stoning and approved their actions (7:58; 8:1) and that his efforts at persecution had the full legal backing of the Jewish authorities (8:3; 9:1f). Thus among his own people, measured by birth, religious upbringing, learning, social standing, and zeal for his ancestral faith, he was second to none.

Then it happened. Was it preceded by a growing awareness of the futility of the law to save (Rom 3:20) and consequently a deepening emptiness within? Or was it the way he saw Stephen dying with such a sense of God's presence and anticipation of heaven (Acts 6:15; 7:55), all that he himself may have been

---

4. Ralph P. Martin, "Peter," in *International Standard Bible Encyclopedia: Volume Three, K-P*, edited by Geoffrey W. Bromiley (Grand Rapids, MI: Eerdmans, 1986), 805.

seeking but never found? Whatever it was, the encounter with the risen Christ on the Damascus road (Acts 9:1–18) set off the seismic shift that turned him completely around.

We sometimes imagine that Paul became the great missionary to the Gentiles overnight. But that is to fail to read the New Testament records properly. After a brief stay in Damascus Paul retreats into neighboring Arabia (Nabatea) (Gal 1:17) for about two years for quiet reflection as well as evangelistic work. Support for the latter comes from the fact that upon his return to Damascus, both the Jews (Acts 9:23–25) and the Nabatean King Aretas (2 Cor 11:32) were out to get him. He then goes to Jerusalem for a brief two-week visit before returning to Tarsus, his hometown, withdrawing into relative obscurity for the next ten years. It is likely that some of the beatings and sufferings in 2 Corinthians 11:23–27 and the ecstatic experiences described in the next chapter (12:1–10) took place during this time. Barnabas then comes along and plucks him out of obscurity to launch him on a wider ministry, beginning at Antioch (Acts 11:25–26). But it would be another two years or so before the church in Antioch sends Barnabas and him out (13:2–3) on their first missionary journey. All these add up to a good fourteen to fifteen years, by which time he was about fifty. Only then is Paul ready for his life work.

There is a lot of talk on promoting younger leaders in the church today. In certain contexts this is surely right because in some places continuing domination by older leaders has stifled innovation and growth. On the other hand, sometimes the push for this has come from ambitious younger people in a hurry. Given these realities, we need to consider carefully before pushing a young person into leadership. It was Dr. Martyn Lloyd-Jones, the great London preacher of the past century, who said, "The worst thing that can happen to a man is to succeed before he is ready."[5] That is probably because he had seen too many young people in leadership roles failing badly. Many would like to hit it big fast, while still young. But God has his own sense of timing. After all, despite his first-rate rabbinic training and theological education, and his obvious leadership gifts, God put Paul through another fifteen years or so of preparation before releasing him for his life work.

But those years of relative obscurity bore rich fruit in Paul's life. Brought up a strict Pharisee, he speaks of his great confidence in being accepted by God on the basis of the law (Phil 3:4–6). But his conversion changed everything. All that gave him his "confidence in the flesh," the basis of his pre-conversion self-assurance, are now completely set aside so that he may find Christ through

---

5. Cited in R. T. Kendall, *The Anointing* (Nashville, TN: Thomas Nelson, 1999), 129.

faith. "Indeed I count everything as loss because of the surpassing worth of knowing Christ Jesus my Lord. For his sake I have suffered the loss of all things and counted them as rubbish, in order that I may gain Christ and be found in him" (3:8–9). The Damascus road experience and the quiet transforming years that followed weaned Paul off all the things that he took great pride in, changing him into a humbler person instead. At the same time, as this and other passages show, Paul's zeal for God, which has been instilled into him from birth and through his upbringing as a Pharisee, remains undiminished. Only that it is now being redirected from glorying in the supremacy of the law to proclaiming "Jesus Christ and him crucified" (1 Cor 2:2).

God's Work of Breaking and Transforming

Based on the above four lives, we can now gather together the threads in our study of God's work in us.

All of us need to go through this process

First, like it or not, if we are to be used by God for his purposes, each of us will have to go through this breaking and transforming process. As noted earlier, sin has left all of us with varying degrees of dysfunctionality. Furthermore, growing up under the influence and pressures of the world around us, consciously or unconsciously we have imbibed much of the corruption and pride of which it boasts. Jeremiah reminds us of this when he told his listeners what God truly delights in.

> Thus says the LORD: "Let not the wise man boast in his wisdom, let not the mighty man boast in his might, let not the rich man boast in his riches, but let him who boasts boast in this, that he understands and knows me, that I am the LORD who practices steadfast love, justice, and righteousness in the earth. For in these things I delight, declares the LORD." (Jer 9:23–24)

In my student days in Australia, we had an old Scottish academic as the warden of one of the residential colleges at the university. He had studied in Cambridge or Oxford, spent many happy years in India, and was now finishing his academic life in Australia. One day, asked by the students about his nationality, he replied without batting an eyelid, "I am a Scot by birth, an Englishman by education, an Indian by culture, and an Australian by contamination!"

Whether we like it or not, living in any environment inevitably results in some degree of influence or contamination by it, large or small. This also applies to our spiritual life, and until the contamination of sin and its power are adequately dealt with, we will not be ready for God's use. For Jacob, God had to take away all the cunning and scheming by bringing him to the point of recognizing that his cleverness will not solve all his life's problems. With Moses, God had to bring him to the point of seeing that worldly wealth, class, and the best of human learning would not take him anywhere close to accomplishing what God had called him to do. Peter the self-made man and born leader had to be brought to the point of realizing that trusting in self and one's innate abilities, however gifted one may be, was a sure recipe for disaster in the work of the kingdom. Paul had to allow his whole understanding of God and salvation to be completely upended, and his confidence in his own efforts to attain righteousness through the law utterly shattered, before God could use him.

In each of the above lives, God took his time. With Jacob it was some twenty years, for Moses forty, for Peter it was three years to begin with followed by many more, and finally for Paul it took some fifteen years. Like it or not, it will be the same for us if we want to be used by God. Despite the demands of our age marked by instant coffee, fast food, and immediate global communications via mobile phones and internet, God still refuses to allow himself to be hurried by our impatience. Why? Because he is determined to form each of us into the image of Christ, in spite of the deep-rooted problems in our lives. God is in no hurry because he cannot. As one preacher once put it, "God took two days to get Moses out of Egypt, but took forty years to get Egypt out of Moses!"

The choice is yours

Some of us are tempted to ask, "How is it that God acts in some lives and then uses them wonderfully for his kingdom purposes but not in others? Does God have favorites?" The truth is that God is actively at work in every life. But the question is whether we want him or not. God does not impose himself on us. Everyone must ultimately make the choice.

There are clear examples in the Bible of people whom God called out for his good purposes but who fail miserably in the end because they refuse to be changed. Samson whom we looked at briefly in chapter 4 is a classic example. Although there was partial redemption at the end of his life (Judg 16:23–30), how much more would he have served God's purpose if he had stopped to listen to God's voice and walk in obedience?

We see a similar story in Saul. Called to be Israel's first king (1 Sam 9:16; 10:1), he started well. But after initial successes he got carried away with power and became careless in the things of God. He unlawfully offered sacrifice when that is a priest's prerogative by law (13:8–15), and then disobeyed God's clear instructions concerning the Amalekites (15:1–35). Despite Samuel's severe rebukes, there was no real repentance. In later years he wasted much of his energy in trying to get rid of his best commander in the army out of sheer jealousy instead of fighting the real enemy, the Philistines. In the end he died a tragic death.

Samson and Saul's lives illustrate so clearly what has often been said concerning the Christian life: "Many start well, but few finish well." If we think that God plays favorites and blesses some but rejects others, we need to think again. Often when faced with difficulties and problems we react with callous indifference to the prompting of our conscience, thus hardening it. Moreover, we turn our anger towards God, blaming him for being unfair or uncaring in our pain. Yet if we would humbly search our hearts, we would find that God has indeed been trying to get to us. But we failed to hear because we have been too busy or stubborn.

God speaks in a variety of ways including through our own mistakes and failures, friends' rebukes and church members' complaints, marital and family problems, crises in our careers, uneasy consciences, and suffering and pain. If we desire God to break and remold us, we need to respond by asking: What is God saying? What is he trying to teach me? As C. S Lewis puts it so aptly, "God whispers to us in our pleasures, speaks in our conscience, but shouts in our pain: it is His megaphone to rouse a deaf world."[6]

Cooperating with God

For God our Father to form us into mature men and women in Christ he needs our cooperation. If that is our desire, we need to ask God for a teachable heart. Invariably that involves recognizing our stubborn pride and where we have gone out of line with his purposes, and accepting that we have messed things up. And the only way forward is through repentance and a complete turning around. But repentance is a hard word!

Many of us have seen numerous young people going into ministry, starting well and making wonderful contributions along the way, only to falter and stagnate later in life. Careful analysis of such cases will again and again reveal issues in each life that needed addressing, but the refusal to accept some home truths about themselves eventually led to long-term failure. That is clearly the case with Samson and Saul, and with Judas and countless others for that

---

6. C. S. Lewis, *The Problem of Pain* (London: Collins, 1957), 81.

matter. What brought redemption to Jacob, Moses, Peter, and Paul was their willingness to accept themselves, their character flaws and failures, as well as their wrong ways of thinking and pride, thus giving God entrance into their lives to bring change. That is repentance.

The willingness to journey together with God also has to be lifelong. When I graduated from university, after wrestling with God for three years in the face of great difficulties, I finally resolved to set aside personal ambitions and respond to his call to the ministry. I thought then that was all that was involved in Jesus's call to self-denial, taking up the cross and following him (Mark 8:34–35; Luke 9:23–24). After all, had I not given him everything he asked? But oh boy was I in for a surprise! As I journeyed, I discover that the call to self-denial and sacrifice is lifelong, and that every day we need to respond afresh to its challenges and demands. And the day we stop walking in step with God, the day we decide to take things into our own hands and deviate just a little bit, that is the day we begin to plateau in our Christian growth. If we are not careful to respond to the Spirit's promptings to get back in line, that will also be the beginning of the end of our usefulness in his service.

Entering Fully into God's Embrace

We have looked at God's work in four lives. But this account of God's gracious work of transformation in human life would be incomplete if we stop here. You may have already noted that in the above stories all four characters went their own way and did their own thing until God stepped in to turn them around. But what if you happen to be one of those privileged ones who learned to walk with God when young and really desire to go as far as possible with him all the way into the years ahead? Or you may be a Christian and sincerely desire to do God's will in life without wanting to wait for a crisis to force you to turn to him. How then would God's work of transformation apply in your case? I believe that the story of Hosea in the Old Testament has something to say to us.

Hosea lived in the northern part of the divided kingdom of Israel and ministered in the second half of the eighth century BC until, probably, just before the capital Samaria fell in 722 BC. The message of the book is centered on Israel's unfaithfulness to the covenant between God and Israel. Israel had turned away from the worship of Yahweh, the God of Israel, to Canaanite pagan practices and Baal worship. Hosea was probably the first to apply the image of spiritual adultery to Israel's apostasy. The thrust of his amazing message was that despite Israel's stubborn unfaithfulness, God remains true to his covenantal commitments even if that requires his redeeming love for her to exceed all human comprehension.

The story begins with Hosea being told by God, "Go, take to yourself a wife of whoredom and have children of whoredom, for the land commits great whoredom by forsaking the LORD" (Hos 1:2). The plain meaning here is that Hosea is told to go and marry a prostitute. If you read commentaries by many modern writers you will find that this simple story in the opening chapters of Hosea gives them endless headaches. Consequently their various attempts at reinterpreting the story according to more acceptable cultural norms effectively distort and reduce the power of the book's message.

Living in my part of the world, one has little difficulty understanding this. In some parts of Southeast Asia, and no doubt elsewhere in the world, it used to be the case (and still is in some places) that girls from poor families in rural areas were contracted out to brothels in the cities by their parents. After some years working in the sex trade, they would bring home their savings, marry, and settle back into village life. Against such a scenario, a plain reading of Hosea's story makes perfect sense. This reading of Hosea is further reinforced when we note that religious prostitution was widely practiced in the ancient world, including in the decadent form of Jewish religion against which Hosea's message was directed.[7] And the significance of Hosea's marriage is the prophetic symbolism by which the prophet is commanded to live out in his own life the message that God has for his people.

Out of sheer grace, God has called out Israel and made her his chosen people. He bound himself to her through an irrevocable covenant, which Hosea's marriage symbolizes. Yet after giving birth to three children, Hosea's wife, Gomer, probably finding life as a prophet's wife rather dull, returns to the supposedly more exciting life of the red lights. At this point God commands Hosea again, "Go again, love a woman who is loved by another man and is an adulteress, even as the LORD loves the children of Israel, though they turn to other gods and love cakes of raisins" (3:1). At great financial cost to himself, and even greater emotional cost, Hosea obeys and redeems Gomer from sexual slavery. And the whole message of Hosea is woven around this story of the prophet's own messed up marriage to a less than worthy woman, who lets him down terribly in spite of all the love he had shown her.

Whenever I come to this story, I ask myself the same question again and again: How do you love a woman (or a man, if the situation is reversed) like

---

7. D. W. Wead, "Harlot; Play the Harlot," in *International Standard Bible Encyclopedia, Volume Two: E-J*, edited by Geoffrey W. Bromiley (Grand Rapids, MI: Eerdmans, 1982), 616–17.

this? How can you? God has taken me through lots of trials and pains over the many years of my life, but I am really thankful that, at least, he never did a Hosea on me! I don't know what I would have done.

Why did God do this to Hosea? As we read further into the book, we begin to understand. Through his own pain, Hosea begins to understand the depth of God's love for his people and the pain within the very heart of God as he calls his people back to repentance and faithfulness. Had he refused God's command to marry "a wife of whoredom" he would never have felt the pain in the depth of God's heart. Only because he obeyed could Hosea's prophecies breathe the incomprehensible tenderness and power of God's love for unfaithful Israel.

> What shall I do with you, O Ephraim?
>   What shall I do with you, O Judah?
> Your love is like a morning cloud,
>   Like the dew that goes early away. (Hos 6:4)

> How can I give you up, O Ephraim?
>   How can I hand you over, O Israel?
> How can I make you like Admah?
>   How can I treat you like Zeboiim?[8]
> My heart recoils within me;
>   my compassion grows warm and tender. (11:8)

> Return, O Israel, to the LORD your God,
>   for you have stumbled because of your iniquity . . .
> I will heal their apostasy;
>   I will love them freely,
>   for my anger has turned from them . . .
> They shall return and dwell beneath my shadow;
>   they shall flourish like the grain;
> they shall blossom like the vine;
>   their fame shall be like the wine of Lebanon. (14:1, 4, 7)

Scholars have noted that never before in the history of Israelite religion had anyone spoken so repeatedly of God's love, and dared to use the language of marital love to describe it. Only because Hosea went through the pains of a horribly messed up marriage, having to bear with an ungrateful and twice

---

8. Admah and Zeboiim are the cities that were destroyed together with Sodom and Gomorrah.

unfaithful wife, could he proclaim the love of God with such tenderness and power.[9]

This brings us back to the point raised earlier. If you desire to walk closely with God from day one, before a major crisis hits you, then you need to be forewarned that the path is not going to be a bed of roses and living happily ever after. If you are seriously wanting to walk with God, you must be prepared to go all the way. And going all the way can bring you into situations that you may never ever have wished for. That is when you find yourself at a crossroads. One way promises comfort and relative ease; the other will upend your life completely. It is at that point that you must choose. And should you decide to back away from the path God has laid out for you, you ought to know beforehand that would mean never arriving at the goal he has purposed for you. You will miss out on God's best for you. How then will you choose?

---

9. See, for example, David Hubbard, *Hosea: An Introduction and Commentary*, Tyndale Old Testament Commentary (Leicester: Inter-Varsity Press, 1989), 26, 29.

9

Servants and Leaders

The central argument in the preceding chapters is that the call to ministry is first and foremost to be servants of Christ in his church. Until and unless this is fully understood, internalized, and lived out in our lives, any talk about leadership roles will almost certainly incur the danger of our being sucked into the quagmire of ambition and self-seeking. Jesus makes this absolutely clear in Mark 10:43–45 and other related passages, which we have looked at.

I am not therefore implying that there is no need for leadership in the church or, for that matter, in the wider world. Indeed, this was what a friend of mine in management consultancy once charged me with after hearing me speak on this subject. Anyone who has read carefully through all the preceding chapters here will know that that is not what I am suggesting.

The Need for Christian Leadership

Earlier we noted in chapter 2, against the backdrop of the leadership malaise in politics, business, and the church in the USA, that Byron Klaus urges Christians in the Majority World to rethink afresh their approaches to leadership in their respective contexts. He is clearly saying this because good leadership is needed for the health and growth of the church. Other Christian observers, including John Stott, have also expressed similar concerns for Christian leadership both in the church and the world.

In his book *Issues Facing Christians Today* Stott titled the last chapter "A Call for Christian Leadership." He begins the chapter by stating that, faced with wide-ranging problems worldwide, "There is a serious dearth of leaders in the contemporary world."[1] The challenges we face include huge global challenges

---

1. John Stott, *Issues Facing Christians Today*, 4th ed. (Grand Rapids, MI: Zondervan, 2006), 485.

such as weapons of mass destruction, the massive economic disparity between North and South, and the environmental crisis; social problems such as race, drugs, alcohol, and poverty; and moral and spiritual concerns including the breakdown of family life, rise of sexual freedom, widespread abortion on-demand, growing materialism, and a loss of the transcendent. Despite the clear danger of impending global disaster, few have answers. "Technical know-how abounds, but wisdom is in short supply. People feel confused, bewildered, alienated . . . like 'sheep without a shepherd.'"[2] Thus there is a great need today among Christians for "more clear-sighted, courageous and dedicated leaders."[3]

From the perspective of Majority World churches, most of the issues raised by Klaus and Stott would apply equally to their situations. On top of these there are a number of other issues that are more particular to church and society in the non-Western world, such as massive corruption. But to go into details would take too much space. I will therefore touch on just one area, the need for men and women in full-time vocational ministry in the church. One problem faced by many churches in the Majority World is that, for reasons of finance and social standing, almost all of our most gifted Christians gravitate towards the professions, academia, or the higher echelons of the civil services in their career choices. Very few willingly give their lives to service within the church. This problem is further compounded by the fact that many who do enter into church ministry often end up going to the West for graduate studies and then do not return to their home countries where they are needed most.

Thus the need for good leadership is indeed a concern of the church worldwide. But is there then a contradiction between the need for leadership in the church and the New Testament teaching on the primacy of servanthood? How do we then reconcile these two apparently contradictory emphases into a coherent whole? This is also related to the question that we touched on in chapter 1: If everyone is a servant, where then are the leaders? The use of the term "servant leader" is clearly not an option. As we have already noted, it is neither a biblical idea nor a helpful one. Is there another alternative?

A Parable out of Auschwitz and Dachau

Victor E. Frankl, the Austrian Jewish psychiatrist, was a survivor of Auschwitz, Dachau, and other Nazi concentration camps. Shortly after his release, he wrote down his experiences and insights gained as a way to help people who are prone

---

2. Stott, *Issues Facing Christians*, 485.
3. Stott, 486.

to despair in the face of difficult and extreme situations in life. At the time of writing, Frankl's book has sold more than twelve million copies worldwide. What surprised him was that the one book, among the dozens he had written, which became a hugely successful bestseller was one that he had originally intended to publish anonymously so that it would not add anything to his personal reputation. Reflecting on this, he tells us in his "Preface to the 1992 Edition" that he repeatedly counsels his students both in Europe and America not to seek success for its own sake. This is because success comes only as a by-product of our commitment to a higher cause apart from ourselves. He writes:

> Don't aim at success – the more you aim at it and make it a target, the more you are going to miss it. For success, like happiness, cannot be pursued: it must ensue, and it only does so as the unintended side-effect of one's dedication to a cause greater than oneself or as the by-product of one's surrender to a person other than oneself. Happiness must happen, and the same holds for success: you have to let it happen by not caring about it. I want you to listen to what your conscience commands you to do and go on to carry it out to the best of your knowledge. Then you will live to see that in the long run – in the long run, I say! – success will follow you precisely because you have *forgotten* to think of it.[4]

Frankl's story is a modern-day real-life parable on the subject of this book. Of course his comment here does not apply in every sphere of human endeavor. But the pursuit of leadership and of success in this world runs parallel to each other and, indeed, often together. And if the arguments in preceding chapters are valid, then what Frankl says about success being the by-product of our pursuit of a higher cause beyond ourselves parallels what I have suggested about Christian leadership at the end of chapter 1. Leadership in the cause of Christ does not come from our striving to be leaders but is the by-product of a life of humble service to him and others.

This is totally in line with Jesus's call to us to discipleship, a journey that also involves our dying to self. "If anyone would come after me, let him deny himself and take up his cross daily and follow me" (Luke 9:23; cf. Mark 8:34). As Dietrich Bonhoeffer puts it, "When Jesus calls a man, he bids him come and die."[5] This dying to self also includes dying to the ambitious hankering

---

4. Victor E. Frankl, *Man's Search for Meaning: The Classic Tribute to Hope from the Holocaust* (London: Rider, 2004), 12.

5. Dietrich Bonhoeffer, *The Cost of Discipleship* (London: SCM, 1959), 7.

after leadership, position, and power. But Jesus does not stop there. He goes on to remind us that, "whoever would save his life will lose it, but whoever loses his life for my sake will save it" (Luke 9:24). Or, as stated in John's Gospel, "Whoever loves his life loses it, and whoever hates his life in this world will keep it for eternal life" (John 12:25).

Applied to the issue of leadership and based on all that we have discussed beforehand, this would mean that if we live by the ways of this world and ambitiously strive for leadership we will end up not attaining it. Even if we manage to get ourselves into some significant leadership roles, we will still fail because our exercise of leadership will be badly compromised by ambition and self-seeking. But if, instead, we learn to die to self and faithfully serve Christ and others, our lives and work will have leadership impact even when we have not sought it.

If Everyone Is a Servant, Where Then Are the Leaders?

This brings us back once more to the question, "If everyone in the church is a servant, where then are the leaders?" The simple answer, as indicated above, is that it is when we live and minister as true servants, our faithful and humble service will impact those around us as great leadership. Leadership is the result of practicing genuine servanthood wherever we are and in whatever position we are called to by Christ and his body, the church.

I suggest that this truth can be better grasped through Martin Luther's concept of vocation (German, *Beruf*) in the Christian life.[6] Luther's view of calling or vocation goes back to our call (1 Cor 7:20; Greek, *klēsis*) to faith in Christ. Being thus called, each of us has an office or station (German, *Amt, Stand*) of one kind or another that defines our relationships to others in this world. Every Christian is called into the kingdom of God and also has a calling in relationship to others in this world. In this sense, there is no one who is not called by God.[7] In fact everyone is called to a number of different offices or stations at one and the same time. For example, a woman is a daughter, a wife, and a mother, a professional, and a member and leader in her church, and so forth.

---

6. I am indebted to Philip S. Watson, *Let God Be God: An Interpretation of the Theology of Martin Luther* (London: Epworth, 1947), esp. pp. 112–16, for what follows. However, Watson's interpretation has been corroborated by other authorities.

7. Luther is making this point in contrast to the medieval idea that vocation or calling applies only to the monastic call.

These offices or stations are the relationships in which we stand to other fellow human beings, and are in Philip S. Watson's words, the "concrete embodiments of the Natural law and its demand for neighbourly love."[8] These are also the vocations and commands through which each of us are called to love and serve our neighbors. As Luther puts it,

> We are to live, speak, act, hear, suffer, and die . . . each one in love and service for others and even for enemies, the husband for his wife and children, the wife for her husband, the children for their parents, the servants for their masters, the masters for their servants, the rulers for their subjects and the subjects for their rulers, so that the hand, mouth, eye, foot, yea heart and mind of the one is also the other's – that means truly Christian and naturally good works.[9]

To sum up, it is precisely in these divinely ordained vocations and offices through which each of us is to fulfill our calling and to love our neighbor. To fail to take our offices or stations seriously is disobedience to the will of God and his commandment.

Applying Luther's understanding of calling or vocation to our discussion, we note that we are called or assigned to different offices in ministry. In whichever office we are called, we are to discharge our responsibilities faithfully in obedience to God's will and in love for our neighbors. In other words, wherever God places us we must carry through our duties as true servants. And in each of these offices, the responsible and faithful exercise of our duties will influence and impact others positively as leadership. Just as Frankl says of success, leadership does not come from our striving after it for its own sake. Rather it happens as the by-product of faithful service to others.

If a man does what a father should do within a family, his service and love for his wife and children will impact the family as a husband and father's leadership in the home; and the same applies for a woman in her calling as a wife and mother. When pastors or ministry workers fulfill their pastoral calling and serve their churches faithfully, members will look to them for pastoral guidance and direction. When a person sitting on the board of a parachurch or mission organization diligently discharges their fiduciary duties as a board member, others in that organization will look up to them as a leader.

---

8. Watson, *Let God Be God*, 113.

9. Cited in Watson, 113.

In each of the above examples, when we serve in a particular office, we are doing no more, but also no less, than what is required of the responsible stewardship of that office. But when we do this faithfully, our lives and ministry become a blessing to others and will bear much fruit for the kingdom. Our faithful and humble service in whatever calling or office God assigns us and wherever he places us will impact those we serve as godly leadership. On the other hand, if instead of serving others, we are always positioning ourselves for advancement and power, others will soon see through us for what we are and reject us as leaders.

There is, therefore, no contradiction between the gospel call to servanthood and the need for real leadership in the church today. Our striving should never be after leadership in itself. Rather, we should be striving to be faithful to our callings or vocations through which we are to love and serve others. Striving for leadership in itself will invariably lead to our being seduced by ambition and power; seeing ourselves as leaders rather than as servants will inevitably result in hubris and an unwarranted sense of self-importance.

Is Everyone Called to Leadership?

If the faithful practice of servanthood leads to leadership impact, does it mean then that everyone is called to leadership? There are three things to consider in answering this.

First, recognizing that leadership take different forms, we begin by asking more specifically whether everyone is called to administrative and organizational leadership. The best place to begin is Paul's Epistle to the Romans wherein he writes:

> Having gifts that differ according to the grace given to us, let us use them: if prophecy, in proportion to our faith; if service, in our serving; the one who teaches, in his teaching; the one who exhorts, in his exhortation; the one who contributes, in generosity; the one who leads, with zeal; the one who does acts of mercy, with cheerfulness. (Rom 12:6–8)

This is one of the lists of spiritual gifts found in the New Testament. What is clear is that Paul tells us that each of us is gifted differently and not everyone in the body of Christ, the church, has the gift of administrative and institutional leadership (12:8; cf. also 1 Cor 12:28). So if we take the biblical teaching on gifts seriously, we will have to say that leadership defined as administrative and organizational leadership is not everyone's forte.

Duane Elmer makes this point emphatically in his book *Cross-Cultural Servanthood*. He quotes Joe Stowell, a past president of Moody Bible Institute, who asserts that at best 20 percent of his students have gifts of leadership.[10] Thus Christian institutions that claim to train almost anyone to be a leader are doing a disservice to the kingdom. He writes:

> Virtually every college major and leadership-development program implies that the graduates will be fit to lead. I find this grossly misleading (pun intended), and it sets people up with false expectation. It is also bad theology since only God bestows leadership gifts (Rom 12:6; 1 Cor 12:4–6). Consequently, many have been trained to lead but are not so gifted, thus creating problems for everyone.[11]

We can now see why Paul prefaced the above passage in Romans with the words, "For by the grace of God given to me I say to everyone among you not to think of himself more highly than he ought to think, but to think with sober judgment, each according to the measure of faith that God has assigned" (Rom 12:3). Because our gifts are different, each of us ought to make a sober judgment, a prayerful and clear-sighted discernment, about what these are and act accordingly. Such judgments are best made together with other Christians in community.

In the context of our discussion, Paul is also challenging us to get out of the hierarchical and positional thinking so common in the world around us. Rather, the concern should be what are my gifts and what role am I to play within the body of Christ. A gifted evangelist or teacher may well be wasting his time and gifts by desiring to be the lead pastor of a big church. Can we imagine, for example, Paul aspiring to be the pastor of a megachurch in Antioch, getting sucked into all its administrative, PR, and funding details, and thereby destroying his brilliant missionary career as a result? And do we want a gifted linguist and Bible translator to take over the running of a huge Bible translation agency and thereby waste her gifts?

This brings us to the second comment. We noted that not everyone has the gift to lead organizationally and we should focus our work in the areas for which we are gifted. But some of us by God's grace have multiple gifts, including that of institutional leadership. This is where, beyond the gifts we have, our

---

10. Duane Elmer, *Cross-Cultural Servanthood: Serving the World in Christlike Humility* (Downers Grove, IL: InterVarsity Press, 2006), 157.

11. Elmer, *Cross-Cultural Servanthood*, 157.

specific calling becomes important. Again, consider the example of Paul. All of us would be tempted to think that with his first-rate rabbinic training he should focus his ministry among his own people, the Jews. Yet, he knew with absolute certainty that his calling was to the Gentiles (Acts 9:15; 22:21). If we are going to be fruitful servants, we must also know our specific calling and follow it wherever God leads.

Earlier we noted the example of E. Stanley Jones who resigned as a bishop-elect of his church a day after being elected. He knew his calling was primarily to be a missionary and evangelist and not a bishop, and he stuck to it. It is not just about gifts, it is also about the prayerful discernment of our personal calling, given the many needs of the church.

In my time I have been privileged to be associated with two different pairs of Christian leaders who had the maturity to live this out. The first pair are two highly gifted individuals who are good friends of each other, and who were both shortlisted by an international organization for the equivalent of the CEO's position. But sensing clearly the Lord's leading and also the needs of his own organization, one of the two candidates willingly stepped aside for the other. Both friends went on to make outstanding contributions in their respective ministries. Again, just recently I had the joy of seeing something similar happen in my part of the world between two other friends who were both front-runners in an episcopal election. One of them, recognizing that the churches in his particular region needed him more, decided to withdraw and supported his friend's candidacy instead. What a blessing it would be to the whole church if such a spirit of servanthood and mutual respect prevails amongst those in institutional leadership!

The third comment is that we have focused our discussion above specifically on leadership understood in a more restricted sense as administrative and organizational leadership. But the idea of leadership also needs to be seen in the broader sense of exercising influence in various form. This has been suggested by, among others, the noted American sociologist James D. Hunter in his book *To Change the World*.[12]

Writing against the backdrop of the "culture wars" in the US, Hunter argues that Christian faithfulness to the creation mandate should not be about "saving Western civilization" or "winning the culture war." Such a concept "of world-changing is oriented towards the idea of controlling history."[13] For Hunter, this

---

12. James D. Hunter, *To Change the World: The Irony, Tragedy, and Possibility of Christianity in the Late Modern World* (Oxford: Oxford University Press, 2010).

13. Hunter, *Change the World*, 95.

kind of talk is too presumptuous because history is ultimately in the hands of God. Instead, he argues that we should be concerned about maintaining a "faithful presence" in this world that is "a recognition that the vocation of the church is to bear witness to and to be the embodiment of the coming kingdom of God."[14] The goal of faithful presence is to work towards realizing God's shalom in all our social relationships and whatever we do, wherever we are.

Critics may disagree with Hunter that any talk about changing the world is too presumptuous, but no Christian would disagree with the fundamental idea of faithful presence. In that sense it is no different from Jesus's metaphors of the church being salt and light in the world (Matt 5:13–16). This is where leadership in the broader sense is required of all Christians since, to the extent that all of us exercise influence in all sorts of different situations, all of us are called to leadership wherever we are. Thus Hunter reminds us that "*the burden of shalom falls to leaders* . . . the obligations of shalom fall to *all of us* to the extent that we wield any influence at all."[15]

Here Hunter is on exactly the same page as Luther. Luther teaches that all of us have a variety of vocations, or offices, that set us in a variety of different relationships and responsibilities to others in this world. In each of these we are to serve and to love our neighbor. To fail to live out our callings or vocations in a responsible manner is to disobey God and his commandments. Hunter takes this one step further and suggests that in every one of these situations or relationships in life we exercise influence. Thus our faithful presence in every situation becomes an exercise of leadership in bringing the kingly rule of Christ and his shalom increasingly into this broken world.

So, is everyone called to leadership? No, if we are speaking of the narrower concept of administrative and organizational leadership. Not every Christian is called to be a church leader, a lead pastor, a bishop, or to lead some major international missions because not everyone is gifted for such organizational leadership ministries. And, if we are not thus gifted, to strive for such positions is sheer folly. In the end we may well end up discrediting ourselves by our administrative incompetence. Even if we are gifted for such tasks, we still need to be sure that we are in the will of God before accepting such a position. This will protect us from being sucked into the quagmire of ambition, as well as reducing our own usefulness through disobedience and failing to go where God wills to send us.

---

14. Hunter, 95.
15. Hunter, 269.

However, understood in a broader sense along the lines of Luther's teaching on vocation and Hunter's on influence, all Christians are indeed called to leadership in the different spheres of influence wherein God has placed us. As noted, only a minority with appropriate gifts are suited and called to institutional or organizational leadership in big churches, whole denominations, or other major ministries. But all of us are called to faithful service in our respective callings or vocations. These may be in situations that are relatively small, private, and unknown – such as caring for our families, welcoming strangers into our homes, or being a friend to neighbors and colleagues in need. We are also called to bear witness to and exercise influence for Christ through our professional working lives. Furthermore, as we have also noted elsewhere in this book, some are called to ministries that carry little or no institutional authority but wherein great influence and moral leadership can be exercised in the church and the world.

Whether we speak of leadership in the narrower or boarder sense, one conclusion is inescapable. Genuine Christian leadership can never be attained by going after it for its own sake; it has to flow out of a life of love and servanthood for our neighbor. As Jesus reminds us, "Whoever loves his life loses it, and whoever hates his life in this world will keep it for eternal life" (John 12:25).

The One Essential Thing – Spiritual Authority

In the above we looked at the importance of gifts in relationship to calling. But we need also to be alerted to a common mistake often made by those in ministry. In the lectures to American theological students that we have already referred to, Stephen Neill reminds us that the possession of great gifts, whether natural or spiritual, does not necessarily make us effective ministers of the gospel. But neither does a seeming lack of special gifts disqualify us from being fruitful. He goes on to assert that "The one essential thing is spiritual power. And that I believe is available to every one of us, if only we are willing to pay the price."[16] Neill is merely echoing here what Jesus said to his disciples just before his ascension: "I am sending the promise of my Father upon you. But stay in the city until you are clothed with power from on high" (Luke 24:49). He then adds whimsically that we can ask of God almost anything we want but

---

16. Neill, *On the Ministry*, 24.

a fair price must be paid because "God is a just salesman; there are no bargain counters in His store."[17]

Neill here is drawing attention to what we looked at in chapters 3 and 4. The importance of spiritual authority and power, so central to the Christian ministry and life, is unfortunately too often overlooked by many today. Much of the modern-day church has become overly dependent on human resources and organization, institutions, money, strategic planning, and the like. Yet we see the indispensable role of the Spirit demonstrated again and again in God's servants and the church, especially in times when the Spirit sweeps through whole regions or nations in powerful revivals.

One of the best modern examples of this can be seen in the history of the Protestant church in China over the past two hundred years. Protestant mission work began in 1807 with the arrival of Robert Morrison, and growth over the next hundred or so years was slow despite the great and valiant efforts of Western missions. John Sung, whom we have already encountered, returned to China in 1927. As he prayed into the matter, God revealed to him the heart of the problem. Western missions had brought in thousands of missionaries, and built many of the finest orphanages, hospitals, schools, and universities in China. And by and large both Western and Chinese leaders were depending on these human resources and not the Holy Spirit for growth. Sometime before his death in 1944, Sung revealed that God had showed him that a great revival was coming to China. But all the missionaries must leave first![18]

Shortly after his death, China was taken over by the Communist in 1949. Just as he predicted, shortly thereafter every missionary was forced to leave. Everything that the Western missions brought was taken over by a hostile government. Most churches were shut down, with thousands of pastors and church leaders imprisoned and the leadership decimated. Church and mission leaders throughout the West saw this as one of the greatest setbacks in modern missions and many feared that the Chinese church had died. What happened next took almost everyone by surprise. Under intense persecution and left with nothing but God, the church suddenly exploded in the 1970s in one of the greatest of modern revivals! As they say, the rest is history.[19]

---

17. Neill, 24.

18. William E. Schubert, *I Remember John Sung* (Singapore: Far Eastern Bible College Press, 1976), 65–66. See also Sung, *Diary of John Sung*, 197–98, 210, 231, 369, 383–84.

19. See, for example, Tony Lambert, *The Resurrection of the Chinese Church* (Wheaton, IL: Harold Shaw, 1994). The Catholic Church has also been impacted by the revival although not to the same extent as the Protestant churches. In 1949, the number of Christians in China were 3,266,000 Romans Catholics, 1,371,000 Protestants (including Anglicans), and ca. 300,000

But spiritual authority is not only seen in powerful revival movements. We also see it when seemingly weak and insignificant individuals are suddenly transformed into remarkable ministers of the gospel in evangelism, church-planting, healing and deliverance ministries, intercession, social outreach, and the like. In our study we have already mentioned some notable examples such as Peter the apostle, the Africans Simon Kimbangu and Prophet Harris, and there are countless others. We will look at just one more to draw our study to a close.

Most of us know Mother Teresa as a world-renowned figure and a Nobel laureate. But what most do not know is that when she started work on 8 December 1949 in the slums of Kolkata (Calcutta), she started as a one-woman ministry, with neither money nor a permanent base. It was not till three months later that she had her first recruit, one of her former students from the private Catholic school where she had been teaching. Her call was to go to "the poorest of the poor, the abandoned, the sick, the infirm, the leprosy patients, the dying, the desperate, the lost, the outcasts" in the slums and shantytowns of the world.[20] Some of her fellow Catholics thought her seriously misguided. One Jesuit commented later, "We thought she was cracked."[21] Yet when she died, India mourned, together with multitudes throughout the world, and accorded her a state funeral.

Much has been written about the social impact of her work in India and elsewhere, and the spiritual and moral influence of her ministry. One of the most penetrating pieces that tells us something of her spiritual authority is penned by Malcolm Muggeridge some twenty-five years after she began her work. He had accompanied her to a New York TV studio for an interview and tells of what happened next.

> I sat in one once with Mother Teresa in New York while she was questioned by a man in a mauve shirt with a drooping green moustache and sad eyes peering out through thick spectacle lenses. Every minute or so he broke off for a commercial. That morning they happened all to be recommending different packaged foods

---

Orthodox (mainly Russians); see also David B. Barrett, George T. Kurian, and Todd M. Johnson, eds., *World Christian Encyclopedia*, vol. 1, 2nd ed. (Oxford: Oxford University Press, 2001), 191. It is difficult to give accurate Christian numbers today but one estimate puts it at 106 million for 2020 (See Todd M. Johnston and Gina A. Zurlo, eds., *World Christian Encyclopedia*, 3rd ed. [Edinburgh: University of Edinburgh Press, 2020], 195).

20. From the "Constitutions of the Society of the Missionaries of Charity," cited in Aikman, *Great Souls*, 220.

21. Cited in Aikman, *Great Souls*, 218.

as being neither fattening nor even nourishing. Mother Teresa, thinking no doubt of the human skeletons she tried to clothe in a little flesh, listened with a kind of wonder, and then, in her soft but clearly audible voice, broke in to remark: "I see that Christ is needed in television studios." Everyone heard her, and a strange silence descended on the studio. I half expected an enraged figure to appear, rope in hand, as he had at the Temple of Jerusalem, to drive us all out into the street. On the previous occasion it was the money-changers; today, the advertisers. Surely he would come, eyes ablaze: You bastards! You and your guaranteed unnourishing bread! In the event, he did not come, but Mother Teresa's words about Christ being needed in television studios, I am sure, continued to echo in the hearts of all who heard them, perhaps serving a similar purpose.[22]

Here we catch a glimpse of the spiritual authority pouring forth from a soft-spoken petite spiritual giant of a woman barely five feet (152 cm) tall. Was there a hidden spring of spiritual power somewhere in her life? Some years after taking her final vows as a nun, Mother Teresa made a further private vow to God, "Not to refuse Him anything." The reason she explained was that "I wanted to give God something very beautiful" and "without reserve."[23] Despite the immense cost involved in the call to serve the "poorest of the poor," she stuck to her vow to the very end, determined never to refuse Jesus anything.[24] Like her Master, she had committed herself to live in total submission to God.

No wonder Malcolm Muggeridge concludes his book on her with this testimony: "I only say of her that in a dark time she is a burning and shining light; in a cruel time, a living embodiment of Christ's gospel of love; in a godless time, the Word dwelling among us, full of grace and truth."[25] And this was a woman without any outstanding gifts by the world's standard and, apart from the formation training of her religious order and a teaching certificate, with minimal higher education. Just as Neill says, we are not disqualified from fruitfulness in ministry even if we have no special gifts – because it is spiritual power that ultimately matters.

---

22. Malcolm Muggeridge, *Jesus: The Man Who Lives* (New York, NY: Harper & Row, 1975), 113.

23. Cited in Brian Kolodiejchuk, ed., *Mother Teresa: Come Be My Light* (London: Rider, 2007), 28–29.

24. Kolodiejchuk, *Mother Teresa*, 331.

25. Malcom Muggeridge, *Something Beautiful for God* (London: Collins, 1971), 146.

This brings us back once more to our theme. The heart of Jesus's authority lies in his submission to his Father. In obedience, he humbled himself as a servant even to the cross. This is also the model for our ministry. Those who have learned to walk in the footsteps of Christ like Simon Kimbangu, John Sung, Mother Teresa, Billy Graham, John Stott, and many others in history know something of the Father's authority through the empowering of the Spirit. Only if we fully understand the meaning of servanthood and submission can we enter into this realm of authority. As Neill puts it so neatly, "God is a just salesman; there are no bargain counters in His store."[26]

Postscript

It was E. M. Bounds who said, "The church is looking for better methods, but God is looking for better men."[27] What Bounds wrote over a hundred years about the incessant search by the church for better methods is nowhere better illustrated than by the church's preoccupation with leadership development courses today. It is also seen in the constant multiplication of church programs and the unending list of "How to" books published everywhere intended to help the church move forward. But one wonders how much these things really contribute to the real advance of the gospel?

To demonstrate this either way will go far beyond the scope of our discussion here. But given the immense challenges posed by the twenty-first-century world, clearly what Bounds says about God's constant search for better men and women is still the urgent need of the hour. Moreover, if my arguments in this book are correct, this also is the central concern throughout Scripture when it comes to God's call to ministry and leadership in the church. Wherever there are those who have walked with him as genuine servants, submitted themselves to his will and discipline, and been transformed by his grace deep within, the work of the kingdom advances because such men and women carry in their lives the mantle of our Father's authority.

---

26. Neill, *On the Ministry*, 24.

27. E. M. Bounds, *Power through Prayer* (1910), reissued by the Christian Classics Ethereal Library, p. 2; https://www.ccel.org/ccel/bounds/power.html.

Further Reading

For readers who wish to pursue in greater detail the biblical teachings on servanthood, church leadership, character, and the like, they can begin with the standard biblical reference works such as the ones listed here.

Bromiley, G. W., ed. *The International Standard Bible Encyclopedia*. Vols. 1–4, rev. ed. Grand Rapids, MI: Eerdmans, 1979–1988.

de Silva, Moises, and Merrill C. Tenney, eds. *The Zondervan Encyclopedia of the Bible*. Vols. 1–5. Rev. ed. Grand Rapids, MI: Zondervan, 2010.

Marhsall, I. Howard, A. R. Millard, J. I Packer, and D. J. Wiseman, eds. *New Bible Dictionary*. 3rd ed. Leicester: Inter-Varsity Press, 1996.

Repeated references are made in this book to persons and churches from the Majority World (Africa, Asia, Latin America, and MENA). Readers who may not be so familiar with the growth of Christianity outside the West should refer to the biographies of specific figures given in the footnotes for more details. To understand the growth of Christianity in the Majority World over the past hundred years, the following books are helpful.

Jenkins, Philip. *The Next Christendom: The Coming of Global Christianity*. 3rd ed. Oxford: Oxford University Press, 2011.

———. *The New Faces of Christianity: Believing the Bible in the Global South*. Oxford: Oxford University Press, 2006.

Sanneh, Lamin. *Disciples of All Nations: Pillars of World Christianity*. Oxford: Oxford University Press, 2008.

———. *Whose Religions is Christianity: The Gospel beyond the West*. Grand Rapids, MI: Eerdmans, 2003.

On the various aspects of the subject of the book, the following is a list of references for further reading, most of which are annotated. These are largely drawn from titles already given in the book. Some additional titles have been included and these are marked with an asterisk (*).

à Kempis, Thomas. *The Imitation of Christ*. Translated by Leo Sherley-Price. Harmondsworth: Penguin, 1952.
Though evangelicals may not go along with some of the author's medieval Christian ideas, many Christians down the ages have benefitted greatly from the book since it was first written in the 1420s.

Atkinson, James. *The Great Light: Luther and Reformation*. Exeter: Paternoster, 1968.
This is a most helpful overview of the history of the sixteenth-century Reformation, conveying with clarity and power the issues at stake.

Augustine. *The Confessions*. Translated and edited by Philip Burton. New York: Knopf, 2001.
Augustine's spiritual autobiography has helped shape not only our Christian understanding of human nature but also Western culture.

Banks, Robert, and Bernice M. Ledbetter. *Reviewing Leadership: A Christian Evaluation of Current Approaches*. Grand Rapids, MI: Baker, 2004.
The authors critically review contemporary Christian approaches to leadership from a biblical perspective. Dissatisfied with the term "servant leadership" they prefer "leading servants" instead.

Bonhoeffer, Dietrich. *The Cost of Discipleship*. London: SCM, 1959.
An important study on discipleship by a modern martyr in Hitler's Germany.

Bounds, E. M. *Power through Prayer*. First published 1910. Reissued by the Christian Classics Ethereal Library. Grand Rapids, MI: Christian Classics Ethereal, 1990. Available online, https://www.ccel.org/ccel/bounds/power.html.
A much-used book on prayer.

*Chandapilla, P. T. *Servant*. Secunderabad, Andhra Pradesh: OM Books, 1999.
A respected Indian Christian leader addresses the same theme of the present volume.

*Chapple, Allan. *Ministry Under the Microscope: The What, Why, and How of Christian Ministry*. London: The Latimar Trust, 2018.
A most helpful exposition of the Bible's teaching on ministry or service which takes an approach very similar to that of this book.

Collins, Jim. *Good to Great: Why Some Companies Make the Leap . . . and Others Don't*. New York, NY: HarperBusiness, 2001.
The product of a five-year empirical research effort by a corporate management research team on how some struggling companies were turned around completely into highly successful ones. The discussion on Level 5 leadership is particularly helpful.

"The Covenant Service." Wikipedia, last modified 4 June 2021. https://en.wikipedia.org/wiki/Covenant_Renewal_Service.
This was drawn up originally by John Wesley in 1755 for the purpose renewing a Christian's covenant with God during the New Year's Eve Watch Night service. The covenant prayer and service are recognized as one of the most distinctive contributions of Methodism to the liturgy of Protestantism.

Drucker, Peter. "Jesus, CEO." *The Economist*, 24 December 2005, 51–54.
The editorial comment sums up the gist of the article: "America's most successful churches are modelling themselves on businesses."

Elmer, Duane. *Cross-Cultural Servanthood: Serving the World in Christlike Humility.* Downers Grove, IL: InterVarsity Press, 2006.
A Trinity Evangelical Divinity School professor brings his background in mission and cross-cultural consulting to bear on the theme of biblical servanthood.

Foster, Richard. *Celebration of Discipline: The Path to Spiritual Growth.* 3rd ed. San Francisco, CA: HarperSanFrancisco, 1998.
Hailed by many as one of the best books on Christian spirituality, it also has two chapters on submission and service or servanthood.

Frankl, Victor E. *Man's Search for Meaning: The Classic Tribute to Hope from the Holocaust.* London: Rider, 2004.
One of the most important books to have come out of World War II by a survivor of the Nazi concentration camps. It demonstrates that it is hope that sustains us in life through darkest despair by giving us meaning and purpose.

Green, Michael. *Freed to Serve: Training and Equipping for Ministry.* London: Hodder & Stoughton, 1983.
A clear and simple introduction to the doctrine of ministry, recalling the church back to New Testament basics.

Greenleaf, Robert K. "The Servant as Leader." Center for Servant Leadership, 1970. https://www.greenleaf.org/products-page/servant-leader-download/.
The original article by the author on the subject; available elsewhere on the internet.

———. *Servant Leadership: A Journey into the Nature of Legitimate Power and Greatness.* New York: Paulist Press, 1977.
The author's more detailed exposition of his view.

Hawthorne, Gerald F. *The Presence and the Power: The Significance of the Holy Spirit in the Life of Jesus.* Dallas, TX: Word, 1991.
A careful biblical and theological study on the nature of Jesus's incarnation and the significance of the Holy Spirit in the human Jesus by a former Wheaton professor.

Hayner, Steve. "Playing to an Audience of One." *World Vision Today* (Summer, 1998): 4–6.
This brief but penetrating article is well summed up by the author's simple statement: "Our ambition is not leadership, but servanthood. Our task is not to grow leaders, but to make disciples who will follow Jesus."

Hunter, James D. *To Change the World: The Irony, Tragedy, and Possibility of Christianity in the Late Modern World*. Oxford: Oxford University Press, 2010.
Written in the context of the culture wars in the USA, the book challenges American Christians to rethink how culture changes in a society and the way Christians should view and talk about their role in the modern world.

*Jacobsen, Eric O., ed. *The Three Tasks of Leadership*. Grand Rapids, MI: Eerdmans, 2009.
Just over one-third of the book deals with servanthood as one of the three tasks of a leader.

Jeremias, Joachim. *The Central Message of the New Testament*. London: SCM, 1965.
There is a whole chapter on Jesus's use of the word *Abba* and what it means for us to know God as Father.

Johnston, Todd M., and Gina A. Zurlo, eds. *World Christian Encyclopedia*. 3rd ed. Edinburgh: University of Edinburgh Press, 2020.

*Kendall, R. T. *The Anointing*. Nashville, TN: Thomas Nelson, 1999.
An important study on the work of the Holy Spirit in God's servants, which is particularly relevant in relation to the discussion on the Spirit's empowering in this book.

Klaus, Byron D. "The Current Flux of Leadership and Emergent Church Models in the USA and Their Transmission Globally." *Encounter: Journal for Pentecostal Ministry* 1, no. 2 (Fall 2004): 25–32.
A Pentecostal leader analyzes and critiques contemporary American church leadership approaches in relationship to similar challenges in the Majority World.

"Leadership Studies." Wikipedia, last edited 2 June 2021. https://en.wikipedia.org/wiki/Leadership_studies.
A useful overview of the current state of leadership studies in the academia and corporate world, primarily in the US today.

Lewis, C. S. *Mere Christianity*. London: Collins, 1952.
A well-known classic and introduction to the Christian faith.

Lightfoot, J. B. *The Christian Ministry*. Edited by Philip E. Hughes. Wilton, CT: Morehouse-Barlow, 1983.
This pioneering essay on patterns of ministry in the New Testament and its developments in the early church has long been recognized as a critical standard on the subject.

Moule, C. F. D. "The Manhood of Jesus in the New Testament." In *Christ, Faith and History: Cambridge Studies in Christology*, edited by Stephen W. Sykes and J. P. Clayton, 95–110. Cambridge: Cambridge University Press, 1972.
An insightful exposition of the manhood of Jesus on how we may understand the profound paradox of Jesus as both divine and human at one and the same time, set against the background of the skepticism of twentieth-century biblical studies.

Neill, Stephen. *On the Ministry*. London: SCM, 1952.
An older book consisting of lectures to theological students that examines various aspects of the pastoral ministry with simplicity and profundity.

*Nouwen, Henri J. M., Donald P. McNeill, and Douglas A. Morrison. *Compassion, Reflection the Christian Life*. Rev. ed. London: Darton, Longman & Todd, 2008.
This book seeks to address the question of what it means to be compassionate in a self-centered, power-hungry world, for "Our God is a servant God."

Nye Jr., Joseph S. "The Benefits of Soft Power." *Harvard Business School Working Knowledge*, 2 August 2004, https://hbswk.hbs.edu/archive/the-benefits-of-soft-power.
A clear and simple exposition on the relative merits of hard and soft power in international relations.

*Osei-Mensah, Gottfried. *Wanted: Servant Leaders*. Accra: Africa Christian Press, 1990.
Reflections on the theme of servanthood in leadership from an African perspective by the first Executive Secretary of the Lausanne Movement.

Packer, J. I. *Knowing God*. London: Hodder & Stoughton, 1973.
A classic and, apart from C. S. Lewis's *Mere Christianity*, probably the most read Christian book in the last few decades.

*Peterson, Eugene. "Followership is Greater than Leadership." In *Letters to a Young Pastor*, Eric E. Peterson. Colorado Springs, CO: NavPress, 2020. Excerpt posted to The DiscipleMaker, 17 June 2020. https://thedisciplemaker.org/followership-is-greater-than-leadership/.
A short incisive piece by a wise pastor and a seasoned teacher of Christian spirituality who feels "that very few people are helping us understand the absolute uniqueness of the way Jesus leads us in this world."

Sanders, J. Oswald. *Spiritual Leadership*. 2nd rev. ed. Chicago, IL: Moody Press, 1994.
First published in 1967, this book by a missionary leader does not seem to age.

Smail, Thomas A. *Reflected Glory: The Spirit in Christ and Christians*. London: Hodder & Stoughton, 1975.
The author shows how the Spirit's work in the human Jesus is intended to be replicated in every Christian so that we will reflect the glory of Christ in life and

ministry. An important study by a Scottish Calvinist seeking to understand his charismatic experience.

Stott, John. *Issues Facing Christians Today*. 4th ed. Grand Rapids, MI: Zondervan, 2006.
A comprehensive overview of the challenges facing the modern church today, especially in the West.

Tan, Siang-Yang. *Full Service: Moving from Self-Serve Christianity to Total Servanthood*. Grand Rapids, MI: Baker, 2006.
One of the few detailed treatments of the biblical view of servanthood on its own terms, not distorted through the lens of leadership.

The Third Lausanne Congress. "The Cape Town Commitment: A Confession of Faith and a Call to Action." 2010. https://lausanne.org/content/ctcommitment#capetown.

Vitz, Paul C. *Psychology as Religion: The Cult of Self-Worship*. 2nd ed. Grand Rapids, MI: Eerdmans, 1994.
A sharp indictment by a Catholic psychologist on the deification of the self in modern psychology and consequently the destructive character of the latter.

Watson, Philip S. *Let God Be God: An Interpretation of the Theology of Martin Luther*. London: Epworth, 1947.
This is one of the better known expositions of Luther's theology though there are many others.

White, John. *The Shattered Mirror: Reflections on Being Human*. Leicester: Inter-Varsity Press, 1987.
The inadequacies of the humanist and modern psychology's views of the human examined from a Christian perspective.

———. *Changing on the Inside: The Keys to Spiritual Recovery and Lasting Change*. Ann Arbor, MI: Servant Publications, 1991.
One of the best treatments on character formation through repentance, sanctification and healing of our inner being.

Yancey, Philip. *What's So Amazing about Grace?* Grand Rapids, MI: Zondervan, 1997.
A most powerful exposition about the meaning of grace in the Christian message.

Langham
PARTNERSHIP

Langham Literature and its imprints are a ministry of Langham Partnership.

Langham Partnership is a global fellowship working in pursuit of the vision God entrusted to its founder John Stott –

> *to facilitate the growth of the church in maturity and Christ-likeness through raising the standards of biblical preaching and teaching.*

Our vision is to see churches in the Majority World equipped for mission and growing to maturity in Christ through the ministry of pastors and leaders who believe, teach and live by the word of God.

Our mission is to strengthen the ministry of the word of God through:
- nurturing national movements for biblical preaching
- fostering the creation and distribution of evangelical literature
- enhancing evangelical theological education

especially in countries where churches are under-resourced.

Our ministry

Langham Preaching partners with national leaders to nurture indigenous biblical preaching movements for pastors and lay preachers all around the world. With the support of a team of trainers from many countries, a multi-level programme of seminars provides practical training, and is followed by a programme for training local facilitators. Local preachers' groups and national and regional networks ensure continuity and ongoing development, seeking to build vigorous movements committed to Bible exposition.

Langham Literature provides Majority World preachers, scholars and seminary libraries with evangelical books and electronic resources through publishing and distribution, grants and discounts. The programme also fosters the creation of indigenous evangelical books in many languages, through writer's grants, strengthening local evangelical publishing houses, and investment in major regional literature projects, such as one volume Bible commentaries like *The Africa Bible Commentary* and *The South Asia Bible Commentary*.

Langham Scholars provides financial support for evangelical doctoral students from the Majority World so that, when they return home, they may train pastors and other Christian leaders with sound, biblical and theological teaching. This programme equips those who equip others. Langham Scholars also works in partnership with Majority World seminaries in strengthening evangelical theological education. A growing number of Langham Scholars study in high quality doctoral programmes in the Majority World itself. As well as teaching the next generation of pastors, graduated Langham Scholars exercise significant influence through their writing and leadership.

To learn more about Langham Partnership and the work we do visit **langham.org**

www.ingramcontent.com/pod-product-compliance
Lightning Source LLC
Chambersburg PA
CBHW072012090426
42740CB00011B/2170